Mick Waters introduces **Jane Hewitt** and

Learning through a lens

It's all about photography

Independent Thinking Press
independentthinkingpress.com

First published by

Independent Thinking Press
Crown Buildings, Bancyfelin, Carmarthen, Wales, SA33 5ND, UK
www.independentthinkingpress.com

Independent Thinking Press is an imprint of Crown House Publishing Ltd.

British Library Cataloguing-in-Publication Data

A catalogue entry for this book is available from the British Library.

Print ISBN 978-1-78135-114-7
Mobi ISBN 978-1-78135-169-7
ePub ISBN 978-1-78135-170-3
ePDF ISBN 978-178135-171-0

Printed and bound in the UK by
Stephens & George, Dowlais, Merthyr Tydfil

For Tony, 'my rock', with thanks for your endless patience, love and support.

Contents

Introduction by Mick Waters

Not many years ago photography was less immediate than it is now. Where people used to take a photograph, wait until the film was used, send away the film for processing and wait for its return to see whether they were satisfied with their effort, they now point and click. They might not even point a camera; a phone or a tablet is waved and the image recorded. Satisfaction or otherwise is addressed immediately and the photo stored or despatched to anyone who might be thought to wish to enjoy it, or it might even be made available on the web to anyone who might come across it. It is virtually impossible to fail at photography; indeed failures are a source of mirth and can be deleted as quickly as they were taken. Some iconic events are viewed through the lens by seemingly everyone in attendance and the image seems as important as the experience.

If only children were encouraged to enjoy writing with such abandon! Have a go, experiment, laugh at mistakes, show people examples you are proud of or your latest effort, comment on each other's … enjoy it! This enjoyment would be a good starting point for in-depth teaching of the power of writing and the ways in which we can get better and better at it. This book uses enjoyment as a starting point and explores in-depth learning by helping the teacher to understand potential and possibility in their teaching.

Jane Hewitt has produced a brilliant book for teachers to show them how they can exploit an interest that pupils will take to naturally. It is a pleasure to introduce her and her work.

As you read this book, you will find ways to build on the strengths in your own teaching. There are ideas, straightforward explanations, extended examples, starting points and helpful suggestions. It is one of those books that you can work through from front to back or you can open it at a particular place to help you though the next part of the teaching repertoire.

The book addresses the subjects of the curriculum. Subject disciplines, and their programmes of study, all contain content which falls into three types of learning. Every subject tries to teach pupils 'how to …' do things; setting out the skills which help pupils to become secure in the subject. Next comes teaching 'about' the subject; exploring and learning the knowledge associated with it. Third comes learning 'through' the subject; learning elsewhere is opened up through proficiency and knowledge.

Jane explores these three areas so well in her book. She offers the teacher the chance to find out how photography works. There is detailed explanation of how the camera works, how to use it well and how to move from being a happy snapper to someone who can compose and structure a photograph that will have real impact.

There are plenty of opportunities for learning about photography. The section on technique covers the 'camera basics' and when this is added to the essence of composition the book moves into the realm of art. The uses of photography as a form of expression, persuasion or investigation will guide you and your pupils into so many subject discipline realms.

Jane brings across the power of photography and offers a rich source of talking points, in depth discussion and debate that can be started in assembly, form time or lessons.

Photography may not be a curriculum subject in the traditional sense but the chance to 'learn through' photography so that it becomes the vehicle for other learning is cleverly presented in the book. Jane manages to offer suggestions and ideas that can be used directly or adapted to bring learning alive for teachers, either by studying with photographs as a resource or by using photography as the touchstone, the hook or the magnet to grab the pupils' attention and take them to new depths in subjects such as science, history or geography. The fascinating practical work on pinhole cameras and camera obscuras, for example, will take pupils into scientific concepts and social niceties of a by-gone historical age. The consideration of apps, iphoneography, and their usage, which flow through the book, will exploit the computer science and technology requirements of a curriculum.

The book offers ways in which difficult concepts in citizenship or PHSE can be addressed through the use of photographs and the engagement of pupils in photography to highlight or exemplify awkward issues. Suddenly the challenge of the embarrassing conversation is eased by the chance to deal with images rather than words. Similarly, concepts that schools often find difficult, such as teaching pupils about protest or campaigning, become more immediate through well-chosen photographs … and Jane offers plenty of those.

By reading the book, you will get to know Jane. She has vast experience as a teacher and knows how to connect with pupils. One connection is through photography. Her professional approach will help you to build upon your own and the ideas, techniques and suggestions will help you to explore learning in new ways, whatever the subject discipline.

Do enjoy this book with the pupils that you teach.

Smile please!

Why photography?

Imagine being told that you could introduce a device into your teaching that was easily accessible and would enable you to be creative. This device comes in a variety of forms and with a range of price tags to suit all school budgets. It will motivate pupils but will also create laughter as well as deep learning and thoughtful reflection. You won't need any real training to use it – you can learn, with your pupils, as you go along. It will allow for mathematical and scientific ideas to be mixed in with art and literacy. And it will stimulate discussion – it may cause controversy, too, but it will certainly get a reaction.

Have I convinced you? Great. But, in fact, you already own at least one of these amazing devices – a camera, smartphone or tablet – so all you need to do is unlock their potential and see how these amazing tools can be used. I hope this book will open your eyes to the ways in which you can use both new technologies and your own skill set to get creative with photography.

Are there skills that you wished you had? I always wanted to be able to draw or play a musical instrument. Sadly, I can do neither. I have tried, really I have, but I was asked to leave the school 'orchestra' at the age of 11 and given the role of stage hand (it still stings even after forty or so years). My drawings look as if a small child has done them and no amount of telling myself, or anyone else, that they are 'abstract' makes them look any better.

Nevertheless, I believe that some skills can be taught and vastly improved by practice. Matthew Syed, in his book, *Bounce* (aptly subtitled *The Myth of Talent and the Power of Practice*) creates a really convincing argument for the power of practice.[1] However, one might argue, as in my case, that if you don't have a modicum of talent in the first place, how can you improve upon it?

Its not what you look at that matters ...
it's what you see.

Henry Thoreau

---

1 M. Syed, *Bounce: The Myth of Talent and the Power of Practice* (London: Fourth Estate, 2010).

Despite not being able to draw, I have always seen myself as a creative person and I would get really frustrated when I had ideas that I wanted to turn into concrete images. Working with children, I know how powerful it is when you can show them examples and when they can visualise their ideas.

My 'eureka' moment came when I was asked by our gifted and talented coordinator to look into buying a digital camera. Following hours of browsing, we spent £350 on a 3-megapixel camera. That in itself shows how quickly technology is moving on. I now have a phone with a 5-megapixel camera and several (OK, loads of) apps that I can use for editing photos.

At the time, my Year 10 form were happy to get involved, so we spent some time just being silly with the camera – striking poses, pulling faces and taking snapshots during form time. The results were amazing and, more importantly, captured what we were doing – you could see the enjoyment, the interaction, the whole classroom experience … The rest, as the saying goes, is history.

If I look back now, the photos are undeniably not my best. Henri Cartier-Bresson talks about 'your first 10,000 images being your worst' and I suppose this goes back to the idea of practice that Syed describes. However, the beauty of photography is that anyone of any age or ability can enjoy and be successful at it.

I was working as an official photographer at a wedding recently when I was approached by an elderly gentleman who pushed his compact camera into my hand and asked me to 'get those lines back'. Following a rather confusing conversation, I realised that he meant the grid on his viewfinder that helps you compose using the

rule of thirds (there is more on this in Chapter 1). If you'd asked him what the rule of thirds was he wouldn't have had a clue, but he did know that those lines helped him and he wanted them back! Instinctively, he was using the tools the camera provided. Having restored his lines, he went away enthusiastically snapping guests, flowers and passing waitresses – a smile on his face and happily interacting with other people, all due to the camera in his hand.

I have no formal qualifications in photography and I am completely self-taught. So, what then makes me think I can write a book on photography? First, this book isn't just about photography – it's about how we use photography to help children to learn. The title 'Learning through a Lens' is what this book is all about. Yes, there are hints and tips along the way, but this is in no way a photography manual.

Second, I have earned my stripes on the teaching front, with thirty years in secondary schools teaching a whole range of subjects and working as an advanced skills teacher for several years. This has given me the chance to work with and learn from some amazing practitioners. I was fortunate, in 2007, to travel to Uganda with some intrepid colleagues and spent two weeks working in schools there. The photographs that I took on this trip showed me just how powerful images can be in learning – some of them appear in this book.

My third justification for writing this book is that what I lack in formal qualifications, I make up for in passion for my subject, a keenness to learn, a willingness to experiment and the solid belief that *anyone* can use photography in their learning – and enjoy themselves at the same time. One of the beauties of photography

Your first 10,000 photos are your worst.
Henri Cartier-Bresson

is that it is subjective. I might like an image, you might hate it – there are no hard and fast rules. I took what I thought was an 'arty' photograph of a bride and groom's feet. The bride, as all brides do, had spent a fortune on her shoes. The groom had been given some socks with camper vans on them. They loved this photo and put it in their album. My mum looked at it and said 'Oh love, you aren't very good are you – you've chopped their heads off!'

Showing children controversial photographs – in the sense that they will elicit a strong negative or positive reaction – can be an effective opener. I often displayed an image on the board when pupils arrived in my classroom, so they became accustomed to coming in and looking for the image. I tried to find photographs that would entertain, shock, have a wow factor – anything that would hook them in. The pupils might well come in and say, 'That's rubbish, that is', but they would at least be forming an opinion. It's like the old joke: how many photographers does it take to make a photograph? The answer is fifty – one to take the photograph and forty-nine to say, 'I could have done that'.

For one starter activity, I displayed *Rhein II*, the image that was sold by the auction house Christie's for US$4.3 million, setting the record for the all-time most expensive photo. This landscape photograph was taken by the German artist Andreas Gursky and is, to my mind, very 'ordinary'. It simply shows strips of grass and water. Yes, I know, it's subjective! (You will have to Google it as I'm not paying for the rights to use an image that I personally don't value.)

I obviously didn't tell the pupils that it was the most expensive photograph ever sold, initially, but I did ask them how much they thought it was worth. This being Barnsley, the first response I got was a very blunt, 'I wouldn't give you ten bob for it, miss.' What ensued was a very heated discussion about the merits of this photograph and the worth or value of photographs in general. It ended up with them all vowing to become photographers as there was obviously 'nowt to this photography lark' and they all fancied making some quick cash! What it showed me was that pupils are often refreshingly honest about

their likes and dislikes when it comes to photography, so any discussion is more about nurturing their own sense of style and creativity than it is about art appreciation.

I believe that photography eradicates boundaries in the sense that it is a great leveller – anyone can take a photograph. Our response to an image is up to us, but the fact remains that the individual who took the photograph is happy with it and so the response of others is immaterial.

Consider the Bill Brandt quote: 'Photography has no rules, it is not a sport. It is the result which counts, no matter how it is achieved.' How amazing is that? There are no rules and you can't get it wrong. You can be as creative as you want and it will still be *your* photograph. You can argue that there are rules – rules of composition such the rule of thirds – but these aren't rules as such; they are just guidelines – rules in name only, which are there to be broken and experimented with.

> *Be daring, be different, be impractical, be anything that will assert integrity of purpose and imaginative vision against the play-it-safers, the creatures of the commonplace, the slaves of the ordinary.*
>
> Cecil Beaton

A smartphone, iPad or camera will enable you and your pupils to utilise all of the suggestions in this book. Photography and photographic devices are creative tools that can be used every day. They are, however, *tools* to use and not an end in themselves. The aim is not to turn you or your pupils into award-winning photographers or for this book to function as a guide to f-stops and apertures. There is some basic information about cameras in Part I, which will form a handy guide as well as pointing you in the direction of more in-depth technical information, but the key focus of this book (no pun intended!) is *learning*. Learning through experimenting, discussing, refining, analysing – learning through a lens!

Photography has no rules.
It is not a sport.
It is the result which counts,
no matter how it is achieved.

Bill Brandt

The book is divided into two main sections:

- Part I: Background and basics. This includes looking at the important functions and settings of cameras, experimenting with photography, the legal position around using images in the classroom and the ethical debates around images, as well as creative ideas which are set outside of the classroom.

- Part II: Projects and applications. In this 'education friendly' section, I present projects focused around street art, miniature figures, visual literacy and challenges, and extended learning opportunities – all designed to be used in a classroom setting and to link with several areas of the curriculum. This section also includes some 'quick wins' – ideas that you could use on development days or in cross-curricular projects.

Throughout the book I have used different coloured boxes to help you navigate the content:

Overview

You will find these at the beginning of each chapter – they will outline the content covered.

Aspects covered

These also appear at the beginning of each chapter – they highlight which curriculum areas and skills are covered.

Help and advice

These provide links back to technical information or advice on how to use your camera or other device.

Tasks

These are ideas for activities linked to a specific chapter but can also be done as stand-alone tasks.

Using photography in learning is so much more than a list of what you could take photographs of. You don't need a book to suggest that you might want to take photographs of your school sports day or end-of-term production. Yes, the basic function of a camera is to take documentary images, but it can be so much more than that. If a camera is used without thought or insight, it becomes another casualty of the technological age. Similarly, an iPad won't make you a great teacher, but a great teacher can do amazing things with an iPad.

The camera itself is just a tool. Just compare the comment, 'That's a great photograph – you must have an amazing camera,' with a comparable one made at a dinner party: 'Thank you, that was a great meal – you must have an amazing oven.' Obvious really – it's the photographer who makes the photograph, not the camera.

> *A lot of photographers think that if they buy a better camera they'll be able to take better photographs.*
> *A better camera won't do a thing for you if you don't have anything in your head or in your heart.*
> Arnold Newman

If you speak to enthusiastic amateur photographers, some will willingly confess that they have 'all the gear but no idea', whilst others have 'no gear' to speak of but have real flair and an imaginative eye. You can find articles on the Internet about professional photographers who have challenged themselves to shoot a whole wedding using just a phone (rather them than me!), but you will also read in Chapter 5 about highly talented photographers who have used their phone to record events in war-torn areas of the world. This begs the questions: is raw talent and having an 'eye' more important than equipment? Is a workman only as good as his tools or can the craftsman create regardless of basic equipment?

The activities in this book don't need expensive equipment – but they do need passion, a sense of fun, a willingness to experiment, to learn on the job, and the ability to see more than just what's around you but to observe your surroundings deeply and with intelligence. I hope that you will be infected with the enthusiasm and passion that photography can bring to life!

The camera doesn't make a bit of difference.
All of them can record what you are seeing.
But you have to SEE.

Ernst Haas

Background and basics

For me photography is to place head heart and eye
along the same line of sight. It is a way of life.
Henri Cartier-Bresson

Chapter 1

Camera basics

Getting started

Before we even pick up a camera, it is important to think about how we 'see' and what actually makes for good composition. Consider the analogy of learning to drive a car: you wouldn't go straight out onto a busy street in your first lesson. You first need to have some understanding of the Highway Code and at least know which pedal makes you stop and which makes you go!

It is interesting that if you give an adult a camera they will often become flustered and worry about which button does what and whether they might accidentally delete something, whereas if you give a camera to younger pupils they will start snapping straightaway – their natural curiosity overcomes any practical fears and worries.

The age of the children you are working with will have a huge impact on your approach to the tasks in this book: working with 16-year-olds on an NVQ course is very different from teaching a Year 2 class. The 16-year-olds may mumble and hang back, pushing their friends forward, saying 'You do it, I'll get it wrong.' The Year 2 pupils will vie for it to be their turn and eagerly volunteer to try things out. The natural curiosity of older pupils is still there, but it is concealed under a veneer of self-doubt and embarrassment. We need to be aware that the fear of looking stupid and of appearing over-keen can dominate their approach.

These ideas may appear to contradict themselves but in fact we need both elements: sometimes we need to just play and accept serendipity – Horace Walpole's 'faculty of making fortunate discoveries by accident', whereas on other occasions we may be looking to create a specific feel or effect and so will need to have the technical know-how to achieve it.

A good way to start thinking about what we can actually see is to use a cardboard viewing frame. You can make your own or pick them up cheaply at a DIY store. Ask pupils to use these in order to become better aware of what they can see when framing an image. They need to learn to think in rectangles! Walk around the classroom, the school, outside, look up, down, close up, far away … This will help with basic composition and make them think before pressing the shutter.

Composition

There are various compositional devices which can be explored and exploited. Some have mathematical concepts behind them, some are creative and others are simply common sense.

Rule of thirds

The first idea to think about in terms of composition is the 'rule of thirds'. Before we go any further, though, it is important to point out that these compositional 'rules' are just guidelines – and that sometimes rules are made to be broken!

Imagine placing a grid of lines over your image to divide it into nine equal spaces. An image is most pleasing to the viewer if the main points of interest are placed at the intersections of these lines. It's a mathematical rule – literally dividing the image into thirds. Most cameras and phones have the facility to display this grid on your screen to help you when composing your photographs. In order to activate the point of focus on a phone, you usually need to tap the screen wherever you want the point of focus to be, otherwise your phone will automatically focus on the centre of your image.

To take a screen shot (such as the image below) on an iPhone or iPad, click the on/off button followed by the main circular button at the bottom of the device.

If you wish to focus on different parts of your screen/image there are two main options:

1   Focus on your primary subject and hold the shutter halfway down – this will lock the focus. You can then recompose using the rule of thirds and place your main object to one side – then press the shutter and take the photograph. Your image will then be pleasingly composed as well as having your main object in focus.

2   If you are using a digital camera which allows for this, you can set the point of focus using your menu buttons.

Other ideas that can be used to improve your composition include:

▪   Leading lines – these are basically anything that 'leads' your eye into the photograph. It could be a road, a fence, a line of trees, etc.

▪   Perspective – remember that you don't always have to look straight at your subject. In its most basic form, do you want a landscape or portrait shot? Try both and see which is the most pleasing. Think about taking shots looking upwards or downwards as it is possible to distort your image and get a completely different effect, or try some 'forced perspective' images.

See Chapter 13: Quick wins
Perspective and forced perspective

▪   Lighting – do you have enough light to take your photographs? Do you want natural light or do you need spotlights and torches to add light to specific areas in your image?

▪   Backgrounds – there is nothing worse than concentrating really hard on your subject only to later notice something in the background of the photograph which ruins the image. The photographer Ernest Haas said that the best wide-angled lens is 'two steps backwards'. Walk around before you take your image – are you in the best position? If you wish, pupils can create their own backdrops by drawing scenes or buildings onto long rolls of paper. You can also purchase ready-made backdrops but these tend to be expensive.

You cannot depend on your eyes when your imagination is out of focus.
Mark Twain

Types of camera

- DSLR – these are advanced and have interchangeable lenses, but can be expensive. If you intend to take up photography as a serious hobby then it is worth investing in a DSLR. The range on offer is literally mind-boggling and you could read reviews for weeks before making a decision. My advice would be to opt for one of the major manufacturers (e.g. Canon, Nikon, Pentax, Samsung). They all have entry level DSLRs which, although expensive, will not break the bank. This will give you chance to practise and to purchase specialised lenses, such as fish-eye, zoom or prime, at a later date.

- Bridge – these are cameras which literally bridge the gap between a DSLR and compact camera. Most are comparable in size to a small DSLR but do not have interchangeable lenses. There are a huge variety of these cameras and their specification will vary depending on the manufacturer and the cost.

- Compact – these are small, light, easy to use and fairly cheap. It would be unrealistic to try and give advice on the literally thousands of models and makes available. These are ideal to keep in your pocket or bag so that you have a camera with you at all times. The low cost of these means they are more likely to be within a school's budget.

- Toy – these are specialist retro cameras (e.g. Lomo Plastic), which use special effects to create stylised images. You can also create toy camera effects by using an iPad and 'toy camera' apps.

- Polaroid – these are now being reintroduced. However, you can also use an iPad and Polaroid apps (see Chapter 4).

- iPhone/iPad – these devices have in-built cameras which can produce reasonable quality images. Apps such as KitCam can give you more control.

Whatever camera you are using, the principles will still be the same. The buttons and dials, however, are another matter – they will be all over the place! However, once you know what you are looking for, a quick look at the camera handbook should show you where to find the correct controls.

As a beginner, you can use your camera in automatic mode, which means that the camera will work out all the settings for you. In some cameras this is a 'P' on the dial, in others a green rectangle. P stands for programmed automatic. If you press your shutter halfway, you will be able to see what shutter speed and aperture your camera thinks is best for a particular shot. This can really help when you first start to use the camera in manual mode as it gives you a useful starting point. In P mode, you can decide on settings such as flash, ISO and white balance (although you can also leave these on automatic), so it's a halfway house between being fully automatic and you deciding upon settings manually.

There are five key aspects that will allow you to take control of your images: shutter speed, aperture, ISO, white balance and metering. Each of these will have an impact upon how your photograph turns out. The effect that you are aiming for will determine which of them takes priority. For example, if you want to freeze the action of a sporting event or wildlife in motion, then you will need a fast shutter speed. If you want your subject in focus and the background blurred then you will be led by the aperture settings.

Auto	Sets everything for you
P	Sets shutter speed and aperture
TV	Shutter speed (you set this, camera then sets aperture)
AV	Aperture (you set this, camera then sets shutter speed)
M	Manual (you set everything)
SCN	Scenes (for particular settings e.g landscape, candle light,etc)

Shutter speed

By taking control of your shutter speed, you can decide what sort of shot you want to take. The higher the number, the faster the shutter speed – for example, 1/200 is one two-hundredths of a second whereas ¼ is a quarter of a second. With a fast shutter speed you can freeze action, and with a slow shutter speed you can create the feeling of movement. Assuming that most people using this book will be shooting with compact cameras or kit lenses, a very general rule of thumb is that you can only shoot hand-held (i.e. without a tripod) at no lower than 1/50 of a second.

If you wish to delve further into shutter speeds, there are hundreds of books dedicated solely to explaining how it can affect your photographs (a good example is *Understanding Shutter Speed* by Bryan Peterson[1]).

Shutter speed experiment

Choose a subject – preferably a static one – and set your ISO (this sets the camera's sensitivity to light – see below) to a fixed amount. If you are inside, set it at 400 and if you are outside set it at 100.

Take several images but each time reduce your shutter speed. So, begin by taking a shot at 1/400, then 1/250, 1/100, 1/80, 1/50, 1/25, 1/15 and 1/4. You will see the numbers change to 0"3, 1", 1"3, etc. which means 0.3 seconds, 1 second, etc.

Print off the images or look at them on your computer – what conclusions can you draw? Which images are darker? Which images are clearer? At what point did your images become blurred?

Next, take two images of water running from a tap. Take one at 1/15 (use a tripod or rest your camera on something) and one at 1/400 – look at the difference in the images.

---

1   B. Peterson, *Understanding Shutter Speed: Creative Action and Low-Light Photography Beyond 1/125 Second* (New York: Amphoto, 2008).

Aperture

The aperture setting allows you to determine how much of your image is in focus. Do you want the whole of your image sharp or do you want the main subject (e.g. a person or flower) in focus and the background blurred? This is referred to as depth of focus or depth of field.

By opening the aperture to its highest setting (e.g. f2 or f1.4), you will let in a lot of light but only focus on a small amount of your image. By using a small aperture (e.g. f16 or f22), you will not let in much light but all of your image will be in focus.

The 'f' number is the aperture – f16 is a small aperture and f2 is a large aperture.

An easy way to remember (even if it's not technically correct) is:

The smaller the number the less of the image will be in focus – but the actual aperture will be wide open so there is lots of light.

Low number **L**ess in focus **L**ots of **L**ight

f2

f5.6

f16

ISO

The ISO button or setting controls the sensitivity to light. If you use a setting of ISO 100 then your image will be sharp and not have any grain (often called 'noise'); however, you need a lot of light for this to work or your image will look dark. Modern cameras can have ISO settings as high as 3200, which will let you take an image without flash in a dark setting, but you will get a very grainy result. Most cameras have an 'auto' setting, so until you are more confident, it is best to leave this as your default setting.

White balance

White balance sets the colour cast for your images – you will have settings for sunny, cloudy, indoors and so on (all with obvious icons of a sun, a cloud, etc.). As with your ISO settings, you can leave this on auto until you become more confident with your camera.

Metering

Metering allows your camera to work out how much light is available – the exposure. If you 'spot meter' it will take a reading from one place (e.g. a person's face) or you can take an overall reading based on however many focus points your camera setting allows, and the camera will give you an 'average' setting.

Additional resources

It may be worth investing in some further resources to develop your work. The following are merely suggestions and are not essential.

- Tripod – if you buy just one extra item, I would recommend a tripod. This will allow you to work on creative images using the shutter-speed setting which will enable you to take photographs in situations where you don't have a great deal of light. It doesn't have to be a really expensive one – if you are using compact cameras you can pick up a mini tripod for a few pounds.

- Card readers or extra camera leads – a card reader will allow you to download photographs from the card in any camera. Prices for these start at £2.99 so they're good value.

- Memory cards – it is helpful to have a couple of spares. Prices vary according to the type of card.

Storage boxes/cases – to keep cameras safe from knocks and dust.

Prop box – develop your own by collecting mirrors, hats, fabric, magnifying glass, jam jars, old CDs, pipettes, plasticine – anything which might be useful.

It is worth pointing out that all cameras will come with a manual, often with online support to help you get started. Sites such as www.photojojo.com also have a wealth of information and exciting projects which are designed specifically for smartphones. The website www.digitalcameraworld.com is in magazine format and offers advice, tips, projects and often free downloads of borders or textures that you can use to embellish your photographs.

Editing software

Once you have taken your images and transferred them to your computer, it is a good idea to back them up onto an external hard drive or CD – it is often impossible to recreate an image if your computer crashes.

There are many photo editing software packages available. Obviously, cost is a factor: while packages such as Photoshop and

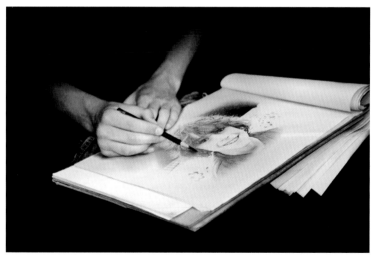

www.photfunia.com

29

Legal issues – an overview

Lightroom are excellent, they are expensive and require training. However, Photoshop Elements is available for under £100.

Windows has some in-built editing functions – if you open an image and then click on the edit tab (in the top left-hand corner), this will open a new window and allow you to carry out some basic edits, such as rotating, cropping, straightening and changing the tones.

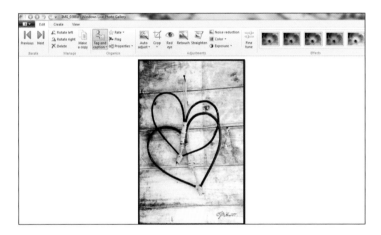

There are a number of free online sites which enable pupils to edit and have fun. For example, www.photofunia.com allows you to place your photograph into different 'settings', such as bill boards, magazine front covers and artist's boards. It is very easy to use and pupils will pick it up almost immediately. This is a good website to use if you have a 'Pupil of the Week' board or page on your blog, as it adds a fun dimension and pupils can then take a copy home as an unusual form of certificate.

The debate around where it is acceptable to take photographs is a complex one but, as a school, you obviously need to decide what constitutes 'responsible policy'. My advice would be that if your photographs are for curriculum-based work, and are being shared just within the school, then your standard waiver is sufficient. However, I would strongly encourage senior leadership teams to involve parents and governors in what teachers are doing – opposition often comes from lack of understanding. In the same way that you have a policy on the responsible use of ICT, which explains the importance of Internet access, Skype, blogging and so on, then explaining why the use of photography supports teachers' practice will hopefully avoid any misunderstandings.

Many school policies in these areas are almost apologetic in tone: they quote the Data Protection Act and are very jargon based. Obviously, the Data Protection Act is important and every school should strive to protect their pupils' rights. However, schools don't send out letters informing parents that pupils will be using chemicals in a science lesson, which could be dangerous if used incorrectly, or that knives could be an issue in food technology lessons, so why would we need one for photography?

However, if you do decide to contact parents, it is important to adopt a positive tone and stress the importance of pupils' learning, with a proviso that obviously the safety and well-being of the pupils is paramount.

A starting point could be:

> *At _____ School we value and celebrate the work of our pupils and want to be able to showcase this. We know that you enjoy sharing in our celebrations and we would like to share our day-to-day work with you.*
>
> *We will be using images created by the pupils themselves in our displays and also via our blogs and website. We are proud of our pupils and their achievements and using photography is a way of allowing us to publicise this. Obviously, we will ensure that sensible and caring protocols will be in place around the use of photographs.*
>
> *We would love you to look at our work, to comment and share. If you have any questions, please feel free to contact us – we would welcome the opportunity to share our ideas with you.*
>
> *Could you please sign below to show that you support us in our work and are happy for your child to take photographs and also to be featured in photographs.*

You are celebrating your pupils' achievements, after all, so there should be no need for you to go into great detail about where images will be stored or about not adding personal details to images. This should all be part of your school ethos: parents should be aware that pupil safety is key, so itemised policies are not what they want or need.

It could be a worthwhile exercise to ask pupils to create this 'policy' and for them to be the ones to illustrate it for parents. Pupils' photographs could be included in the policy letter as examples of good practice so parents can see the policy in action.

Can I use images that belong to other people?

The copyright of any image belongs to the photographer and you may not use that image or alter it in any way without the photographer's permission. Many teachers do not seem to be aware of this – how often have you seen a presentation which includes an image with a copyright watermark embedded across the middle? This is breaking the law – not to mention how unprofessional it looks. You may have also been at presentations where the image used has been enlarged and become pixelated – thus rendering it worthless. The photographer will have uploaded a small image file to the Internet precisely to stop people from using their work without permission.

So, how can you find amazing images that you *can* use in your lessons or presentations legally? It is easier than you think and you will be surprised at the quality and wealth of materials that are available. Any media that is marked as having a Creative Commons licence is useable in education.

First, you need to understand the concept behind the Creative Commons. There are six basic types of licence. Some will allow you to use, alter and redistribute the image, even for commercial purposes. For example, the image below is licensed under CC-BY-3.0

If you are only using the images within the classroom, and simply using them, rather than editing or Photoshopping them, you can basically use any image that is marked as 'for use' under a Creative Commons licence. Here are some of the different types of image you may encounter:

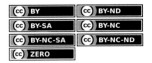

CC-BY	Creative Commons – BY If you use this type of image you must attribute it. This means that you must say who took the photograph and who it belongs to. BY applies to all of the licences. There are no other restrictions so you can build on the image, change it and even use it in a commercial project.
CC-BY-SA	Creative Commons – BY-ShareAlike This is exactly the same as CC-BY, but if you change the photograph you must license this 'new image' in the same way as the original, i.e. ShareAlike.
CC-BY-ND	Creative Commons – BY-No Derivatives You can use this image in any way you like as long as you attribute it and do not make any changes.
CC-BY-NC	The same as CC-BY but you cannot use the image for commercial purposes.
CC-BY-NC-SA	The same as CC-BY-SA but you cannot use the image for commercial purposes.
CC-BY-NC-ND	The same as CC-BY-ND but you cannot use the image for commercial purposes.

You will probably never need to refer to this table, unless you decide to publish work that you have created from other images.

To make it really easy to find images without checking individual licences, you can use the search facility at http://search.creativecommons.org/ which allows you to search for the sort of licence you need. For example, the image below is licensed under CC-BY-3.0.

If you just want images or videos for classroom usage, simply untick the two boxes at the top and type in your key word – try Fotopedia to begin with as these tend to be images from semi-professional or professional photographers who are willing to share their work.

If you want to check out the quality of the images available, go to Fotopedia and, as a starting point, look at the amazing images provided by NASA. However, be warned: this has a tendency to become addictive and you could lose several hours of your time before you realise it!

Camera basics glossary

Key word	Definition
Aperture	How wide the shutter is open. This can alter how much of your image is in focus. This is shown as 'f' numbers – f16 is a small aperture and f2 is a large aperture.
Auto mode	Setting which means that everything is 'set' for you – the equivalent of point and press.
Bridge camera	A bridge between a compact camera and a DSLR – it has some of the advantages of a DSLR but is often less expensive.
Card reader	Device which allows you to transfer photographs from your camera's memory card to your computer.
Compact camera	Small lightweight cameras with an in-built lens and no additional lenses.
DSLR	Digital single lens reflex camera – it has interchangeable lenses and can be expensive. For the more experienced photographer.

Key word	Definition
Forced perspective	A technique to alter the way we see a person or object (e.g. by placing them in the distance to create optical illusions).
ISO	Light sensitivity
Leading lines	Lines which lead your eye into a photograph (e.g. a winding road or a row of trees).
Manual	You decide upon all the settings – aperture, shutter speed, white balance, ISO and metering.
Memory card	Storage device inside your camera (the digital equivalent to film). Available in different formats (e.g. CompactFlash, Secure Digital) depending on the make of camera. Remember to 'format' this occasionally when in your camera as this will clear the card completely and keep it from becoming cluttered.
Metering	This allows you to set for light in different parts of your image – you can use spot metering, centre weighted or evaluative meter settings.

Key word	Definition
Perspective	The way you look at something – the angle or viewpoint from which you take your photograph.
Polaroid	Camera (or app) where the photograph is printed instantly.
Rule of thirds	A compositional device where you divide your image into three both horizontally and vertically. The points of interest would be placed where the lines cross.
Shutter speed	The amount of time the shutter stays open. Setting button 'S' or TV (Canon). A fast shutter speed will freeze action but allow in less light. A slow shutter speed will blur motion (but will require a tripod).
Toy cameras	Retro cameras (often plastic) which all have differing special effects, such as colour leaks.
White balance	This affects the colour cast of your photograph. Settings such as 'sunlight' or 'cloudy' will help to capture true colours.

The painter constructs, the photographer discloses.

Susan Sontag

Overview

Soap film/bubble images

Experimenting with paint

Bokeh

CDs and water droplets

Aspects covered

Science – light/strength of solutions

DT – incorporating designs into objects

Music and science – what does music look like (using paint and speakers)

Chapter 2

Experimental photography

The beauty of experimental photography is that you can't get it wrong. It's abstract, it's conceptual, it's basically playing! Some results have more of a wow factor than others, but because it is all subjective, it is very low stress. It is also often messy so protective clothing may be a good idea for some of these activities.

Soap film/bubble images

Ingredients

- 1 bottle of bubble solution (you can buy this from any toy store or supermarket) or make your own using washing-up liquid – it will need to be a concentrated solution
- 1 bottle of glycerine (this is used in baking so you should find it in supermarkets)
- 1 bubble wand – or one wire coat hanger bent into a loop
- 1 flat-bottomed container
- 1 dark background – black paper or a black towel
- Natural sunlight or a torch

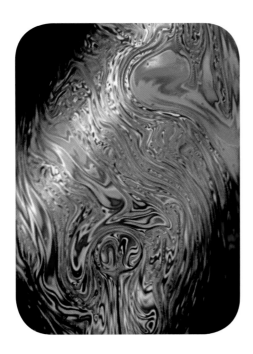

Method

■ Mix the bubble solution with a teaspoon of glycerine (this helps the soap solution to stay on the loop for longer) in the flat-bottomed container.

■ Dip the bubble wand into the solution then shake it until it is covered in a film. Lift gently and hold still – the solution will begin to 'settle' and colours will start to appear.

■ By tilting the wand slightly, into the light or away from the light, you will get different effects and colours.

■ You can vary the effects by the amount of light, the position of the wand and the angle of the camera.

■ If the solution seems fairly strong (you can always add more glycerine) you can blow on it slightly – this will cause a different effect.

Variations

■ Try making different shaped wands using wire coat hangers or pipe cleaners – can you make a square bubble? Can you design a pyramid shape? How does it affect the colours and patterns? You could use this as the basis of a science experiment and look at the different types and strengths of bubble solution as well as the shapes and sizes of the wands.

■ Try blowing on the bubbles to which glycerine has been added and photograph them as they float.

■ Set your camera to a fast shutter speed in continuous shooting mode and capture the bubble as it bursts.

See Chapter 1:
Camera basics
Using shutter speed

■ Buy or make a huge bubble wand – take this outside as it tends to get messy. Pupils will have to factor in weather conditions when they take their photographs, especially wind speed and direction.

■ Aim to take a photograph of a whole bubble showing the reflections in it. This will involve thinking carefully about where to take the image and what will be reflected in the bubble. The example on page 40 was taken in an enclosed area with glass bricks which caused wonderful colours and shapes. You can also see the reflection of the group of photographers.

If your camera has manual focus, it might be better to use this – otherwise the camera may focus on the loop itself and not the bubble solution.

Editing

- Crop a section of your image so that you are left with just the pattern (i.e. cut out the loop) – you can use any photo editing software to do this (see Chapter 1).

- Edit the image by over-saturating the colours in Photoshop or another editing program such as Snapseed (see Chapter 4).

- When you have found an image that you like, use it to create a design for an object that could be sold, such as a mug, t-shirt or card.

- Send your image to one of the poster sites on the Internet and have a huge one printed for your classroom wall.

- Put your best images into a slideshow to be used as wallpaper or screensavers for your class computers.

See Chapter 1: Camera basics	See Chapter 4: iPhoneography and apps
Editing software	Apps

Experimenting with paint

Martin Klimas is a German artist who wanted to find out what 'music looked like'. He achieved this in an amazing series of images. He set up a speaker with a Perspex sheet on top covered with different coloured paints – then turned up the volume. The photographed results were stunning.

Look at the images in the Telegraph picture gallery.[1] Play the tracks Klimas used and ask the pupils which image they think are which songs. Perhaps you could have a joint art/music/science/photography project to recreate these images.

Hindu festival of Holi

Holi is a religious festival which celebrates good overcoming evil and the arrival of spring. It is a vibrant and colourful celebration which involves much throwing of powdered paint – there are some amazing images on the Creative Commons website. I've always wanted to get a group of pupils dressed in white in an open space with a white canvas or sheet on the floor and allow them to throw paint while other pupils and myself photograph them. Alas, I have not yet been that brave – but if you are, send me some images!

See Chapter 1: Camera basics
Can I use images that belong to other people?

---

1 See <http://www.telegraph.co.uk/culture/culturepicturegalleries/9113526/Photos-of-paint-splashes-in-mid-air-by-Martin-Klimas-show-what-music-looks-like.html/>.

Bokeh

Bokeh is a Japanese term for the out-of-focus areas in a photograph. It comes from the Japanese word 'boke' which means haze. It often manifests as circles of light in the background of an image. It is a pleasing and deliberate blur rather than just an out-of-focus photograph.

Bokeh is created by using an aperture setting of f1.4 or f2.8, which allows the main part of the image to be in focus whilst the background is blurred and out of focus.

> **See Chapter 1: Camera basics**
> Aperture and depth of focus

You can experiment with different filters which will turn lights into shapes. You would normally need a filter kit and an expensive fast lens with the ability to take photographs at a wide aperture, as in the image on the left. However, there is a way to create your own Bokeh images without spending a great deal of money (although ideally you need a DSLR camera which allows for manual focus).

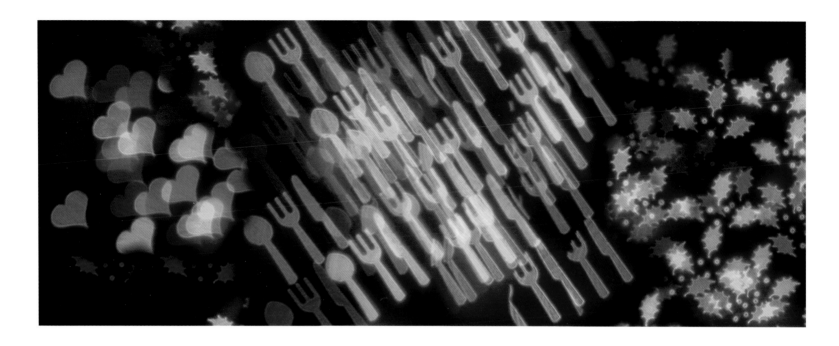

Ingredients

- DSLR camera with manual focus

- Fairy lights – you can buy these from supermarkets for less than £2 at the right time of year

- Thin black card or paper

- Decorative hole punches *or* a craft knife and clip art shapes

- Rubber bands or masking tape

- A darkened room (all teachers should have one of these to lie down in occasionally!)

You can create your own bokeh filters either by cutting shapes into black card or working with your DT department and using laser cutters.[2]

See Chapter 1:
Camera basics

Shutter speed

ISO

Additional resources

2 See <http://www.diyphotography.net/diy_create_your_own_bokeh/>.

Method

- Create your filter from a hole punch and black card.

- Cut the card into a circle which is 5 cm bigger than your lens.

- Place the card in front of the lens and carefully secure with a rubber band or masking tape.

- Tape the fairy lights to a plain wall in a random fashion but not too far apart.

- Set up your camera – if you have a tripod, you can set the camera to a shutter speed which will allow in enough light. You will need to experiment, depending on how much light there is in the room.

- Set your focus to manual (it will be set as auto as default) – the switch is usually on the lens itself.

- Focus on the lights – by moving the lens and yourself you will eventually find the 'spot' where your lights are focused and actually become the shape that you have created from your black card. You may need to move around and experiment with the distance between you and the lights.

- You can then edit images into collages or cards.

CDs and water droplets

If you hold a CD up to the light and move it around you will get some amazing rainbow streaks of light. By working in pairs, pupils can tilt the CD into the light to achieve some simple but very effective photographs. If you drop water droplets onto the CD using a pipette or a straw, it is then possible to see images of the light reflected in the water drops.[3]

If you want to take it even further, you can create the image in a fairly dark space and shine a torch over the CD – this will produce light streaks, bubbles with light reflected in them and trails of light from the torch!

> Create tutorials for bokeh, soap bubbles or CD and water droplets using a mixture of text, images and video.
>
> **You could use apps such as Explain Everything or Creative Book Builder.**

---

3   For some examples see <http://photoextremist.com/how-to-take-psychedelic-photos-of-cds/>.

For me the camera is a sketchbook, an instrument of intuition and spontaneity.

Henri Cartier-Bresson

Chapter 3

Camera obscuras and pinhole cameras

Camera obscuras

The term 'camera obscura' comes from two Latin words. It literally means 'dark room': camera – room/chamber and obscura – dark. In very basic terms, a camera obscura works like a pinhole camera – that is, a sealed light-free box or room with a blank side at one end and a tiny hole at the other. There are various camera obscuras in the UK that you can visit – the most famous being in Bristol, Edinburgh and Aberystwyth.

It became obvious to people way back in history that they could see images on walls. Tracing these back to their source, they realised that small holes in the rock were allowing light through and it was this light that was creating the image. In *100 Ideas that Changed Photography*, Mary Warner Marien describes it as 'the odd phenomenon of an inverted image projected on an interior wall' which 'intrigued ancient thinkers in Europe and Asia.'[1]

In the fifteenth century, Leonardo da Vinci became fascinated by how the eye worked and did several experiments on eyeballs, pickling and then dissecting them. He drew links between the way that light travelled through the pupil and produced a 'flipped' image, in exactly the same way that the camera obscura (although it wasn't called this until much later) projected an upside-down image onto a wall

1 M. Warner Marien, *100 Ideas that Changed Photography* (London: Laurence King, 2012), p. 8.

through a pinhole. He said: 'No image, even of the smallest object, enters the eye without being turned upside down.'

The camera obscura is a very simple device which can be created in a dark room in order to project the image from outside onto the opposite interior wall – albeit upside down and flipped horizontally. There is obviously a great deal of scientific and investigative work involved here, so it would make a great project to link the arts and science sides of the curriculum.

The law of optics

Light travels in a straight line. When the rays are reflected from a bright subject and pass through a small hole, they do not scatter but cross and reform as an upside-down image on a flat surface opposite the hole.

The camera obscura works on the same principle as the pinhole camera (see page 50) but it can be great fun because you can use a room to create it – and so pupils can be actually inside the camera itself! It is not a traditional type of camera, in that you can't capture the image it creates – unless you draw over the image or take a photograph of the image with a modern camera.

If you decide to try and build a camera obscura, you may be tempted to order a kit from the Internet. My advice would be, don't – it's a total waste of money. It will consist merely of sheets of black sugar paper, a 6 x 4 photo mount (about 99p from most stationers), white sheets of paper, a strip of Velcro and a plastic lens – all of which can be readily and cheaply purchased.

Location

You need to find an area which has as few windows as possible, a wall opposite the window which is fairly clear and a lively scene outside the window (e.g. people or traffic) which will be projected onto the wall. You could set finding a suitable location as the original brief for your pupils as it is actually quite difficult to find a space which meets all of the criteria.

Resources

- Blackout paper (e.g. black poster/sugar paper)
- Masking tape
- A compass (or similar) to make a hole

Windows are always much larger than they appear when you are trying to cover them completely, so don't underestimate the time or the amount of black paper and tape that it will take to cover them.

Optional resources

▨ If you don't have a white wall you will need a plain white sheet or white paper to cover the wall.

▨ You will need a camera which allows you to set exposure times and a tripod (if you want to photograph the image).

Ideas

▨ Give pupils the words 'camera obscura' and nothing else – see where they go with it.

▨ Hand out a sealed parcel which contains the words 'camera obscura' and a pile of black sugar paper plus a pin and a roll of masking tape. On the outside of the parcel, place the words 'special task' and 'handle with care'.

See Chapter 4: iPhoneography and apps

▨ Give half the pupils the above and the other half cameras/iPads/videos to make time-lapse movies of how they get on.

If money and permission were no object, what would you like to turn into a camera obscura?

▨ If money and permission were no object, what would you like to turn into a camera obscura? Write a brief from a fictitious TV company which wants to make an educational video explaining what a camera obscura is, how it works and how to make one. You will find examples on the Internet.[2]

One development from the idea of a room as a camera obscura is to try and make this 'portable', so people have tried using sedan chairs or tents. Following on from this, the camera obscura became a box rather than a room, and these became the forerunners of the cameras that we now use today.

---

2   For example: <http://www.howcast.com/videos/387145-How-to-Transform-a-Room-into-a-Camera-Obscura/>.

Pinhole cameras

Photographer Justin Quinnell created his own portable camera obscura – which he wears on his head – using a laundry basket, shower curtain and dustbin lid! He calls this the 'I-Scura' and he created it to wear at festivals.[3] Show this to pupils as an example of just how creative they can be. Justin is a 'pinhole photography master' and examples of his work can be found online.[4]

Building your own camera is not only a great way to learn the true basics of photography, it is also incredibly fun to create something from scratch that can take a photo.

G. Fabbri, M. Fabbri and P. Wilkund[5]

The pinhole camera uses the same basic principles as the camera obscura: it is a light-sealed box which has some form of light-sensitive material at one end and a hole at the other. You can use a small box or even a can to create your own. By taping waxed translucent paper over the end of your 'camera', you should be able to see the image.

It is also possible to use light-sensitive photo paper as an alternative to the waxed paper (or tracing paper) – both will display your image. You can use actual film but this can be fiddly and needs to be inserted into the 'camera' in complete darkness.

You can buy pinhole kits online.[6] And if you would like your pinhole camera to look more like an actual camera, use the free downloadable templates from Corbis.[7]

---

3 See <http://petapixel.com/2013/07/04/a-diy-camera-obscura-you-wear-on-your-head/>.

4 See <http://www.pinholephotography.org/>.

5 G. Fabbri, M. Fabbri and P. Wilkund, *From Pinhole to Print: Inspiration, Instructions and Insights in Less Than an Hour* (Stockholm: Alternative Photography, 2009), p. 3.

6 For example <http://photojojo.com/store/awesomeness/diy-camera-kits/>.

7 See <http://www.creativetechs.com/iq/free_pinhole_camera_templates_from_corbis.html/>.

Instructions

- Take a clean cardboard box or tube with one open end – make sure that there are no holes or seams where light can get through.

- Pierce a small hole in the closed end.

- Cover the open end with tracing paper (or similar) and secure.

- Sit in a dark room and place a blanket over your head.

- Hold the 'camera' at arm's length – with only the pinhole section outside of your blanket – facing a light source.

- The image should be projected onto your tracing paper (backwards and upside down).

Explanations as to how to make a pinhole camera from a Pringles tube can be found online.[8]

If you want your 'camera' to actually record images, place light-sensitive paper (you can purchase this on the Internet) on the opposite side to the pinhole. Make sure that you insert this into the 'camera' in a dark room or cupboard.

Discussion

- What containers could you use to create a pinhole camera?[9]

- What effect does the length of time you allow light into the camera have on your image?

- What effect does the shape and size of the pinhole have on the image?

- What could you use to cover the pinhole and effectively close your shutter?

---

8 See <http://scienceforkids.kidipede.com/biology/animals/nervous/doing/pinholecamera.htm/>.

9 For some suggestions visit <http://www.diyphotography.net/23-pinhole-cameras-that-you-can-build-at-home/>.

The world's largest photograph

The world's largest photograph was created as a result of the Legacy Project in Southern California in 2006.[10] It took a team of six people two months to prepare and create the image. The pinhole camera was installed in an abandoned jet hangar, Building 115, and the final image was 110 feet wide and 32 feet high. The image was projected onto light-sensitive muslin and is officially – according to the Guinness Book of Records – the largest photograph in the world.

The team had to deal with various issues, such as getting permission to use the building, ensuring it was completely free from light and making sure they had the exposure timings correct for the light-sensitive material. They faced the logistical problems of sourcing a seamless piece of material to project the image onto and finding machinery which would enable them to reach the top of the hangar to seal gaps that were allowing in light. They knew that they only had one chance to get this right, so they had to make sure they had checked and solved any problems before actually starting to take the image. There is a video which explains what they did and how they solved the issues,[11] but this would be a good practical problem for pupils to work on as a thinking skills exercise.

Having watched the video, what questions would pupils ask of the people who worked on the project?

---

10 See <http://legacyphotoproject.com/>.

11 See <http://www.youtube.com/watch?v=Nc-79vOzshw/>.

> If you were going to create a pinhole camera in an empty aircraft hangar, (45 feet high and the distance from your pinhole to the material is 55 feet), what problems might you face and how would you solve them?
>
> Prompt words for potential problems: size of building, how to seal light leaks, what to project onto, how to make your 'screen' light sensitive, cost, exposure, storage/display of image, sourcing materials.

Creating a pinhole effect with software or apps

It is possible to create a pinhole effect using software and applying a vignette and grain or 'noise' to your image. However, you will need more expensive software such as Photoshop to do this. Some modern compact cameras have 'art filter' settings and you will find pinhole is one of these. The image below right is an example of this.

You can also use apps to create a pinhole effect. Pinhole HD costs less than one pound and has three basic 'films', which include a black-and-white option. You can take a single exposure or a double exposure to give you the movement associated with a pinhole image. The vignette of the pinhole is added automatically.

Original

Noise   Vignette

Vignetting refers to a fall off in brightness towards the edges of a photograph in order to emphasise the centre of the image. *Noise* is the grain (a variation of brightness or colour) which is apparent in an image if the ISO is high.

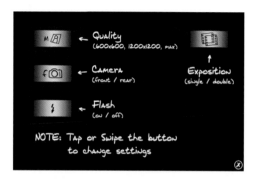

Pinhole effects using the app Pinhole HD

World Pinhole Photography Day

The last Sunday in April is World Pinhole Photography Day. There is a dedicated website and any images taken with a pinhole camera on that particular day can be uploaded to the site.[12]

According to the organisers, World Pinhole Photography Day was set up to 'celebrate the joy of simple creativity using the medium of lens-less photography'. The goal is to show that from something as simple as a cardboard box with a tiny hole, it is possible to create inspiring images.

There is an online gallery of images from the previous year which is organised by country. In 2012, there were 3,426 images from seventy-five different countries. The range of images is amazing and there are obvious links to the geography curriculum. The website contains a wealth of information, including tips on how to create your own pinhole camera.

Register at www.pinholeday.org and upload an image from a camera that you have created yourself.

12 See <http://www.pinholeday.org/>.

Chapter 4

iPhoneography and apps

The word 'iPhoneography' has been coined to cover the taking of photographs with an iPhone, but as many schools now use iPads and other such devices in classrooms, I'm sure you can stretch the term to include these activities in your work.

We are all well aware of the good use that can be made of apps in the classroom. However, there are literally hundreds of thousands of them, such that it would be impossible to keep up to date, even in just the area of photography. In June 2012, there were over 700,000 apps in the iPhone App Store (according to www.about.com) and around 10,000 photography-related apps. The apps included in this chapter are simply some examples of ones that are reliable, easy to use and either free or inexpensive.

Professional photographers usually work on image manipulation software such as Photoshop or Lightroom, but these cost many hundreds of pounds – whereas the app Photoshop Express is currently free from iTunes. This means Photoshop is now available for schools to use cheaply and easily. But this is just one example – there are many apps that will allow pupils to create effects with a couple of clicks which would previously have taken years of training in complicated software.

Look at your phone – how many photographs do you have stored on it? I would guess that some are imported from your computer, some are taken specifically on your iPhone or iPad (Photo Stream now syncs these) and some may be screen shots of things that you've found whilst browsing on the Internet or recommendations from Twitter. All of these images are at your fingertips and immediately accessible.

As a result of this accessibility, photography has changed so much that it is almost a different art form from what it was several years ago. The immediacy of photography is obvious in world events – for example, according to Phil Coomes, the BBC's picture editor: 'Photographers working for the newswire agencies supplied the BBC with more than 4,000 pictures of the funeral of Baroness Thatcher, each one arriving minutes after it was shot.'[1]

> Document a key event in school or your local community using only iPads or iPhones.
>
> Create an immediate 'newsroom' style display board – make this a working display.
>
> Create a blog page with images which summarise a particular event.

I can't resist saying here that I think that schools are wrong to ban the use of mobile phones. They are amazing tools – just like iPads and other forms of new technology. We simply need to agree with our pupils that we are going to use them thoughtfully and carefully. I remember, years ago, battling with my ICT coordinator to be allowed to use e-mail in the classroom. We had linked up with a school just outside New York and the pupils wanted to exchange letters and questions. I was overruled and had to spend many hours copying and pasting pupils' letters into a Word document that I could attach to my e-mail. Sounds ridiculous now, doesn't it – a bit like it will in years to come when teachers laugh at us for blocking powerful new technologies. As one Twitter user percep-

tively observed: 'If pupils are misusing technology in your lesson you have a behaviour problem not a problem with technology.'

> Use an iPad to take images of your class throughout the week. Create a storybook of your week using apps such as Comic Life. There are tutorials and examples available on the associated blog.[2]

Apps

The best thing about apps is that they have an 'undo last step' button – wouldn't it be great if life had that? The iPhone (1st generation) was released in 2007 with a 2-megapixel camera, the specification increasing with subsequent releases. As a result, iPhoneography has become an art form in its own right. In her introduction to *The Art of iPhoneography*, Stephanie Roberts claims that it 'can help you practice spontaneity and loosen up the traditional approach to photography'.[3]

Photographers have shot whole weddings using only iPhones, and there are books, blogs, Flickr groups, competitions and awards for iPhone photography. You can buy lenses (starting at £5 instead of hundreds of pounds for the equivalent SLR lens), tripods,

---

1   P. Coomes, Thatcher's Funeral: The View from Above, *BBC News* (23 April 2013). Available at: <http://www.bbc.co.uk/news/in-pictures-22225122>.

2   See <http://blog.comiclife.com/>.

3   S. C. Roberts, *The Art of iPhoneography: A Shutter Sister's Guide to Mobile Creativity* (Lewes: Ilex Press, 2011), p. 7.

remotes and filters for your phone, in the same way that professionals would have bought for their cameras fifty years ago. This trend has brought photography into the everyday sphere and introduced a fun, spontaneous element.

Reproduced by permission of Balazs Gardi/Basetrack.

In 2011, *The Guardian* reported on two war photographers, Teru Kuwayama[4] and Balazs Gardi,[5] who were documenting events in Afghanistan using camera phones and the app Hipstamatic.[6] Although they both had a range of camera gear and lenses, Kuwayama said they used the iPhone because 'it was the ideal, rugged piece of gear' – it allowed them to move about easily, didn't attract dust and forced them to get closer to subjects. He added: 'The iPhone is this ubiquitous thing that everyone has got in their pocket' and that it fitted with 'our idea of demystifying journalism'.

This is just for fun and the only limits and constraints are your imagination:

Design the camera of the future. Explain how we will take, process and produce images in the future – be as creative as possible.

---

4 See <http://terukuwayama.com/>.
5 See <http://www.balazsgardi.com/>.
6 War Photography? Isn't There An App for That? (7 July 2011). Available at: <http://www.guardian.co.uk/media/2011/jul/06/afghanistan-war-iphone-images>.

The important thing is not the camera but the eye.
Alfred Eisenstaedt

What can apps do?

Having taken your image, what can you do with an app, or what do you want an app to do? The main features that most photography software will cover are the ability to:

- Crop – cut unwanted sections out of your photograph in order to focus on a key area

- Rotate – change the orientation of your image

- Change the colour or desaturate it (make it black and white)

- Alter the hue and saturation

- Add a filter

- Add a texture

- Add an effect (e.g. Grunge, Vintage)

- Add a border

- Add text

- Create a collage

- Save/share/print

See Chapter 10: Photo challenges

Create a 'good app guide'

Some apps are designed for specific purposes whereas others will do all of the above. The ones below are simply examples of the types of app available.

HOPE Poster Photo Filter

The famous 'Hope' poster, which became the iconic image of Barack Obama's 2008 presidential campaign, is instantly recognisable. It was designed by Shepard Fairey (originally a graffiti artist) and is a stylised stencil portrait which uses three colours – red, blue and beige. It has the single word 'Hope' typed at the bottom.

1   2   3

The HOPE app recreates the stencilled image using three colours from any of your photos. First, open an image and choose a style. Next, select a word to go with your image and type. You can also choose 'expert' mode which allows you to alter the strength of each colour, but the presets usually give pleasing results.

HOPE?

SECRETS

DECAY

JOURNEY

TIME

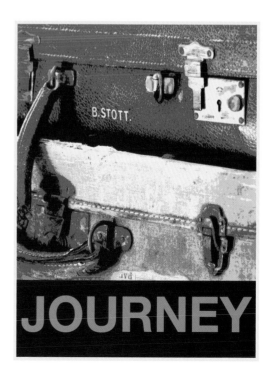

JOURNEY

Ways to use this app

- Create several Hope-style images of your own but don't add the text. Ask the pupils to work together and agree upon which word they feel best describes the image and then justify their choice.

- Use the images on page 63 with the words removed to do the task above.

- Use the images on page 63 but leave the words on for pupils to evaluate and see if they agree with the choice of word. Can they think of a better alternative?

- Use the images on page 63 to create a six-word story which should include the word on the image. For example, a story for the top-left image could be: 'Job lost, life on hold, hope?' Or 'Invisible to all. Hope all gone.'

- Is the word 'Hope' the best fit for this image? What alternatives would pupils suggest?

- Imagine that the images on page 63 represent book covers. Write the 'blurb' which goes with the book. What is the book about? What about key features, characters and plot? You could give pupils a set number of words to help them focus their efforts. Model this as a whole class and then get the pupils to write their description in pairs.

See Chapter 7: Visual literacy

Six words – one photograph

- Set pupils to work in groups to generate a set number of words which convey emotions. They should then choose one of these words and create an image to go with it. They can then upload it to the HOPE app and print out their image. You can then create a classroom display of all their words.

- Organise pupils into groups, as in the activity above, but ask them to choose a word from the list below (words could be put into a bag and drawn out or uploaded to a random picker such as www.classtools.net).

Time	Peace	Hope
Fear	Listen	Trust
Bravery	Journey	Friendship
Sadness	Forget	Regret
Joy	Love	Read
Forgiveness	Secrets	Question

iLapse

There are several time-lapse apps, some free and some paid for. The one I'm using here is called iLapse and is currently £1.49. You can have so much fun with this app. It does basically what it says – takes hundreds of photos and then seamlessly puts them into a movie which plays at 24 or 25 frames per second.

You input into the app:

◼ How often to take a frame (photo).

◼ How many frames to take.

◼ What speed to play the movie – i.e. how many frames per second.

The app then calculates how long your movie will be when complete.

There are lots of opportunities for maths here. For example, you could ask pupils how many frames they would need to take if the frame rate is one every ten seconds and you want the session duration to be one hour. You can deepen this activity by looking at the length of the final video – for example, if it is created at 24 frames per second ask pupils how long it would take to film, or if we want a finished movie of 10 minutes and our frame rate is one every 20 seconds, how many frames will they need? The possibilities are endless. The good thing for you, as the teacher, is that the app will automatically do the calculations and show these at the bottom of the screen!

Ways of using time-lapse apps

◼ To make a stop-motion type film. Create figures using Fimo or Plasticine, or use Lego figures or toys. Move the figures between each frame. This takes a lot of patience, hand–eye coordination and team work. One pupil should be put in charge of watching the counter to shout 'now' every time another frame is taken.

◼ To film a lesson. A frame every 10 seconds for 360 frames will give you a session duration of one hour. The final movie (at 24 frames per second) will be 15 seconds long, so you could show this as a plenary at the end of the lesson. (No, I didn't do those calculations manually!)

When you are creating something as a class (e.g. the photo booth activity in Chapter 13), it is a great way to record your work.

To record yourself putting up a display, teaching a PE lesson, the school entrance hall, birds in the nature area, traffic outside of school – the possibilities are endless.

> Take images of yourself during a week and turn these into a 'diary' using a suitable app of your choice.

WordFoto

WordFoto is a brilliant app which allows you to turn your photographs into an image made from words. You can choose which words to use and also which style of image you want to create.

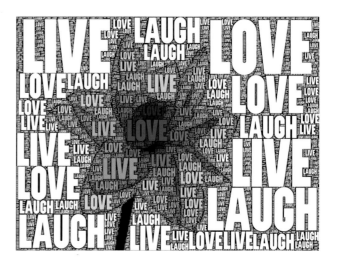

The app often works better if the image has few colours and a well-defined outline, so you will need to experiment. A bold effect has been achieved in this daffodil image which has a clear outline and very little shading.

> See Chapter 7: Visual literacy
>
> Ideas for using images and words

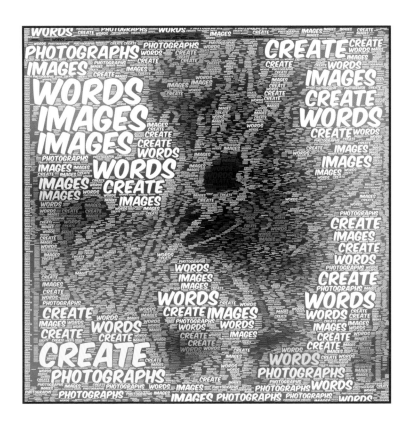 

The app 'WordFoto'

The words used in this image were 'words', 'photographs', 'create', 'images' as I was just using it as an example. If you gave pupils an image, they could decide on six or so words that really sum it up. For example, this could have been 'petal', 'stem', 'leaf'. Use this as an example and then allow pupils to choose their own image. The image could be an iconic figure, a diagram or a famous site. Pupils will have to decide which words and which style work with their images.

Snapseed

Snapseed is an image-editing app which costs a fraction of the price of professional editing software but still produces impressive results. There are hundreds of apps that perform basic editing functions such as cropping, adding filters, lightening/darkening and sharpening the image – it is a case of personal preference. Snapseed, however, is easy to use and produces pleasing results. It will perform the obvious edits but these additional functions are useful:

- Drama – this can 'rescue' an underexposed image or give real punch to a bland one. It can also create stylised effects.

- Vintage – this will add one of several vintage washes, such as authentic scratches, and allows you to alter the strength of the added texture (see the image on page 69).

- Grunge – a stronger filter than Vintage but it creates some striking effects, which can be varied.

- Black and White – this gives you several presets such as 'bright' or 'film', which give a different feel to images.

- Tilt Shift – this allows you to take a photograph (urban scenes usually work best) and tilt it so that it looks like a 'miniature' scene.

- HDR Scape – this allows you to add a high dynamic range (HDR) filter, which creates dramatic images by allowing you to brighten dark parts of an image without washing out the lighter areas.

- Frames – this offers a range of over twenty frames (e.g. black and white but with different effects) which finish off your photograph and give it a more professional feel.

Menu

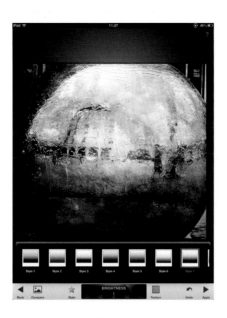

Vintage

Grunge

Textures

Examples of multiple filters and frames

ToonPAINT

ToonPAINT is an excellent app to use in the classroom as it allows you to turn your images into a cartoon – enabling you to create storyboards of work. You might want to take photographs of pupils in a series of freeze-frames to tell a story. You could use them in Writing to Instruct by creating a sequence of images for an instruction sheet, which could be anything from 'How to make cupcakes' to 'How to be happy'!

The app is simple to use and allows you to alter the strength of the black outlines and the colour. You can easily create your own images to use as writing or discussion stimuli using this app.

Other apps which are worth a look include:

- Graffiti Me – this turns your images into graffiti and allows you to add different colours, wall textures and text.

- Haiku Deck – this allows you to produce a very professional looking presentation. It is also very easy to use.

- Photo Slice – this allows you to slice your photograph into segments (like a jigsaw), as well as turning part of it into a sketch. It is good for presentations or for dividing photographs between groups.

- Vintique – this has a range of antique and retro style filters as well as several useful borders.

■ Over and Quipio – these apps enable you to place text over images to make pleasing posters.

■ Strut Type – this will recreate the look of an old photograph, including mould and mildew, so it is good for creating historical-type images (see also the section on aged photographs in Chapter 13).

■ Polaroid Instant – this allows you to create an old-fashioned Polaroid-style photo, complete with distinctive square format and white borders.

Millennium bridge   Polaroid instant   London

This is a 'fun app' which allows you to load your photograph into a 'camera' – it then recreates the old style Polaroid cameras and prints out your image. You can then add effects and texts. The size and border are both the same as a 'traditional' Polaroid camera

■ Hipstamatic – this allows you to 'play' with different lenses, films and flashes. Some effects come with the app but others need to be purchased separately.

■ Pic Grunger – this applies a whole range of grunge filters and effects.

■ Comic Life – this is invaluable for enabling pupils to create their own comics and stories (see Chapter 9 for some examples).

■ Ripped – this allows you to turn part of your photograph into a sketch, as if it's been ripped out (see Chapter 7 for some ideas).

■ Apps Gone Free – this app isn't specifically photographic but it does inform you about which apps are free on a daily basis, so you can pick up some really good resources for free.

■ Instagram – this is different from an app because, as well as allowing you to add a whole range of retro-style filters and borders to your work, it enables you to upload your images for others to comment on and share via social media or e-mail. Photographs are cropped to a square format.

■ Guardian Eyewitness – this shows you just one amazing photograph from the news on a daily basis and includes a description of the image and who took it. If you tap the 'info' button, it gives you a photography tip based around the image. Often this is connected with which unique features made the photograph worthy of being an 'image of the day', such as demonstrating good composition or scale or why certain exposure times have been used.

This chapter is never going to be complete as new apps are being created constantly and updated regularly, so I would encourage you to let your pupils experiment and play!

Instagram

May 2013

The best thing about a picture is that it never changes, even when the people in it do.

Andy Warhol

Chapter 5

Ethics in photography

Photojournalism

A subtitle to the first part of this chapter could actually be: 'Should these photographs have been taken?' Having concentrated on practicalities and how exciting photography can be, we also need to be aware that there is a flip side to photography – just as important, but deeply emotional in nature.

We live in a digital age where images are beamed almost instantaneously into our homes. As I write this chapter, horrific images are being broadcast of the bombing of the Boston Marathon. They are heart-wrenching and graphic but they also tell the world what is happening. If we had simply been told that a bomb had gone off, would we have understood in the same way without the images? Or were the images too explicit and upsetting to have been shown?

Choose one image from today's newspapers (or you could use an online news site) which sums up the 'world today' in your opinion. Justify your choice to a partner.

One image which sums up this debate is the Pulitzer Prize-winning photograph by Kevin Carter. It was taken in the Sudan in 1993 and depicts a vulture that appears to be waiting for a starving child to die. It has been described as 'a picture that stunned a somewhat complacent world'.

© Kevin Carter/Corbis.

In interviews, Carter stated that he waited about 20 minutes for the vulture to spread its wings. When it didn't, he took this photograph and chased the vulture away. The image was first published in the *New York Times* and prompted many enquiries as to the fate of the child. The newspaper subsequently ran an editorial in which they claimed that the child had 'walked away from the vulture but that her eventual fate was unknown'.

The questions raised by this photograph are manifold, but the image itself portrays a stark reality: children in the Sudan were dying from malnutrition. Did the world need to know and was this image an effective way, or the best way, of conveying that?

Philosophy for Children

According to Sapere, Philosophy for Children (P4C) aims to encourage children 'to think critically, caringly, creatively and collaboratively'. It is based on pupils generating their own philosophical questions around a given stimulus (in this case an image) and deciding, as a group, which question to use as the basis for their discussions.

Exemplar questions from past sessions using Kevin Carter's photograph have been:

- Should the photographer have taken the image?

- Should this photograph have been awarded a prize?

- Would knowing what happened to the child make a difference to our feelings about the image?

The section on SIFT (in Chapter 9) has further guidance on analysing images.

The P4C discussions could be run simply using the image or the following ideas could be introduced into the pupils' debate, as and when you feel it might be appropriate:

- Journalists and photographers in the Sudan at that time had been told not to touch famine victims because of the risk of disease, so Carter was just following instructions.

- Carter has been heavily criticised and referred to as 'another predatory vulture' on the scene.

- Carter won the Pulitzer Prize for this image.

- Carter was suffering from depression and committed suicide three months after the photograph was taken.

- The vulture has been used both as a symbol of oppression and as representative of government.

- At the time the image was taken there were relief workers in the area.

- The girl's parents were receiving food from a UN plane and they later returned for their child.

- The publicity generated by this photograph has been immense – because of this image the world became aware of the famine and atrocities in North Africa.

- The girl was obviously very weak – Carter could have infected her and any food given to her could have been too rich and caused an adverse reaction.

- Carter waited 20 minutes before taking the photograph.

- This image moved many people to donate, so effectively saved the lives of many children.

These statements could also be distributed to pupils for them to analyse as part of their debate. Cut up print-outs of the text and hand them out randomly – ask pupils to introduce their statement when appropriate into the discussion. In doing so, they may actually have to argue a point of view which is different to the one that they actually believe in, thus encouraging them to explore an issue from more than one perspective.

One key question that this photograph raises is: does the world need to see shocking images of this nature? In their preface to the harrowing book, *The Bang-Bang Club*, which tells the story of four photographers (including Kevin Carter) who covered apartheid in South Africa during the 1990s, Greg Marinovich and João Silva pose a question about the morality of their work: 'When do you press the shutter release and when do you cease to be a photographer?'[1]

The book is a challenging and often uncomfortable read because it is a graphic account of horrendous acts of violence. Yet the underlying question remains: without the photographers and journalists, atrocities will continue, so do photographers have a responsibility to share these images with the world? At what point do the images become unacceptable? If the images are unacceptable, surely that means

---

1 G. Marinovich and J. Silva, *The Bang-Bang Club: Snapshots from a Hidden War* (London: William Heinemann, 2000), p. xiv.

that what is happening is unacceptable. Are we deluding ourselves by insisting that if we can't see it, then it's not that bad?

On a forum discussing Kevin Carter's photograph, one person had written: 'Sometimes I want to ask God why he doesn't do something about world hunger – I don't because I'm afraid that he might ask me the same thing.' Whilst this led to a discussion about the existence of God, which is not the issue here, it did lead to a lot of posters on the forum basically saying 'don't criticise the photographer if you aren't doing anything about world hunger yourself'.

If shocking photographs are splashed across the media every day, are we sensationalising events to such an extent that we eventually become immune to distressing images? Questions about the newspaper censorship of images that are too graphic to be shown raises questions about the media making decisions for their readers that are perhaps not theirs to take. Ask the pupils what they think about these issues.

> 'The camera never lies.' Discuss.

In *The Bang-Bang Club*, Marinovich says: 'It had been the first time that I had seen a person killed and I could not shake off the feeling of guilt that he had died so close to me that I could have reached out and touched him, yet all I had done was take pictures.'[2]

2   Marinovich and Silva, *The Bang-Bang Club*, p. 30.

Is there a line that should not be crossed? Who makes the decision – the photographer or media outlets? Photographers put their lives at risk to take these images, so how important is photojournalism to our understanding of our world?

Photojournalists Tim Hetherington and Chris Hondros were killed in Libya in 2011 whilst covering the revolution to overthrow Muammar Gaddafi. Hetherington's last photograph was, ironically, a helmet with a bullet hole in it. It *suggested* violence rather than portraying it in a graphic manner and has been described as 'typical of his style of work'. Tributes flooded in after their deaths, which caused many war photographers to question what they were doing and some to stop altogether. In his article 'Revisiting Memory and Preserving Legacy', Peter van Agtmael claims that 'For war journalists, the fascination with war is largely defined by a powerful curiosity about death.' He goes on to question why people would 'risk death to make peace with it.'[3]

Are we right to combine this with the idea that if we show an event, we are celebrating it? If we ignore what is happening, are we condoning it? If we represent shocking incidents visually, will people understand what they are seeing? There are no obvious answers

3   P. van Agtmael, Revisiting Memory and Preserving Legacy: Tim Hetherington and Chris Hondros (18 April 2013). Available at: <http://lightbox.time.com/2013/04/18/revisiting-memory-and-preserving-legacy-tim-hetherington-and-chris-hondros/>.

to these questions, but they do provoke some useful thinking for young people.

The inspirational photographer Don McCullin was the first photojournalist to be awarded the CBE. His powerful black-and-white images of Vietnam and the conflict in Northern Ireland communicated the stark reality of these situations. He says: 'It is the photographer's job to show some of [the horror of war].'[4]

In his article, 'Don McCullin: My Last War', Anthony Loyd says that 'his photographs burnt their way into my mind's eye like the lasting impression of a light bulb on the retina.'[5] If nothing else, that powerful description of the effect of photographic images of war will give you an amazing starting point for discussing this issue. McCullin is quoted as saying: 'Photography for me is not looking, it's feeling. If you can't feel what you're looking at then you are never going to get others to feel anything when they look at your images.'[6]

In many interviews, McCullin talks candidly about the agonies and the risks involved in taking many of his images, observing that 'you live with your conscience'. In 2013, he was one of the judges in the Faith through a Lens competition, which sets out to 'uncover personal experiences which can be shared through the medium of photography'.[7]

Is McCullin's involvement in this competition a way of reaffirming the compassionate side of human nature rather than the violence of war? In an interview with Jessica Bracey in *Photography Monthly*, he states: 'Being aware of the world sharpens the mind, the eyes and the senses. I had a disability and I overcame that through photography.' The fact remains though that, as he says, 'Good news never sold a newspaper.'[8] This could form the basis for another philosophical discussion around the subject of disturbing photojournalism.

After the 9/11 attacks on the twin towers in New York, there were many harrowing images – a girder transformed into an iron cross, lone figures covered in dust, single shoes, hundreds of photos pinned to railings with appeals as to the whereabouts of missing loved ones, the dirty streaked faces of fire fighters.

4   Quoted in D. Clark, Casualties of War – David Turnley – Icons of Photography, *Amateur Photographer* (27 February 2010). Available at: <http://www.amateurphotographer.co.uk/how-to/icons-of-photography/535927/casualties-of-war-david-turnley-icons-of-photography>.

5   A. Loyd, Don McCullin: My Last War, *The Times Magazine* (29 December 2012). Available at: <http://www.thetimes.co.uk/tto/magazine/article3638191.ece>.

6   D. McCullin, *Sleeping With Ghosts: A Life's Work in Photography* (London: Vintage Press, 1994), p. 96.

7   See <http://www.faiththroughalens.co.uk>.

8   J. Bracey, The War on Film, *Photography Monthly* (11 October 2012). Available at: <http://www.photographymonthly.com/Magazine/Photography-Monthly-articles/Interview-with-photography-legend-Don-McCullin>.

One image, however, caused more uproar than others: *The Falling Man*, which showed a man jumping to his death from the North Tower of the World Trade Center. It was taken by Richard Drew, an Associated Press photographer, and it won a 2001 World Press Photo award. A documentary, *9/11: The Falling Man* (2006), was made about this one image, what it portrays and whether or not it should have been published.

As it became obvious that escape was not possible from the Twin Towers, some desperate people actually jumped. This image showed an almost silhouetted man falling head first to his death. It is not known for certain who the man is, although some people have claimed that he was Jonathan Birley who worked on the top floor of the North Tower. The man in the image has made a choice – admittedly a horrific choice – about *how* to die, rather than whether to die, but in the image he appears to be dignified in his pose.

The image caused many people to question whether it should have been published on the front page of newspapers and sparked a debate about whether it was 'too gratuitous for public consumption'. Richard Drew, however, argues that the image is a 'quiet photograph' and has none of the violence associated with other iconic images of assassinations and attacks. Tom Junod, writing for *Esquire*, observed: 'If he were not falling, he might very well be flying.'[9]

When interviewed, Drew said that this image will always be a part of him: 'Even if people don't want to see my photograph, that man did fall out of the building.' He added: 'To me, he'll always remain the unknown soldier.'[10]

There is something poignant in an 'ordinary' person becoming an 'unknown soldier' and representing the many who have died. The changing of the guard at the Tomb of the Unknowns in Arlington National Cemetery, in Virginia, and the haunting sounds of the Last Post at the Menin Gate Memorial, in Ypres, commemorate the courage of the unknown soldiers who gave their lives so bravely. Do we owe it to these people to remember, in whatever way we can? Alternatively, do we need to preserve their dignity and censor certain images?

Some commentators have claimed that by both taking and reproducing this photograph, the falling man is being stripped of his dignity and his death has been turned into a voyeuristic act. Hundreds of distressing images and footage were taken on 11 September – can we say that some were acceptable to be shown and not others? Where do we draw the line?

> Can you name five things that you *couldn't* photograph?

---

9   T. Junod, The Falling Man, *Esquire* (8 September 2009). Available at: <http://www.esquire.com/features/ESQ0903-SEP_FALLINGMAN>.

10 J. Pompeo, Photographer Behind 9/11 'Falling Man' Retraces Steps, Recalls 'Unknown Soldier', *Yahoo! News* (29 August 2011). Available at: <http://news.yahoo.com/photographer-behind-9-11-falling-man-retraces-steps-recalls-unknown-soldier.html>.

Compassion fatigue

If we look at the gallery of winners from the World Press Photo awards, many of the titles give us an insight into the violence contained therein: 'Gaza Burial', 'Collaborator', 'Battle to Death', 'Pepper Spray', 'El Salvador Gangs'. Some of the images are graphic, some are moving; all are incredibly sad. Do we just accept that the world in the twenty-first century is violent, or do we still have a reaction to these often horrific images? And what of the photographers who frequently risk their lives to show us these images?

As a child growing up in the 1960s and 1970s, I was made aware of starving children in West Africa. Images of malnourished Biafran children appeared on the news and we were told not to waste food. There were adverts on TV and in magazines showing seriously ill children with distended stomachs. Westerners became so familiar with such images that we were perhaps at risk of becoming desensitised to their powerful content.

In *Compassion Fatigue*, Susan Moeller talks about the 'power of images'. She says the first time we see an image in an ad campaign about starving children we are 'arrested by guilt', the second time we linger for a while but then turn the page, and the third time we turn the page quickly. Finally, the image or advert is viewed with cynicism or as 'an attempt to manipulate'.[11]

It is interesting that, in describing this subject, I would like permission to use the Kevin Carter image of the young child and the vulture, but I am unsure about the falling man. Is that me censoring this book according to my views? One benefit of living in the twenty-first century is that you could now go and Google this image and find it easily within a couple of clicks, so is 'censorship' the wrong word or the wrong choice? Should we use all images, however shocking, to try to educate people? Can we assume that individuals will implement their own personal censorship?

---

11 S. Moeller, *Compassion Fatigue: How the Media Sell Disease, Famine, War and Death* (London and New York: Routledge, 1999), p. 9.

Advertising campaigns

Analyse the leaflets, posters or advertising campaigns from different charities – for example, Barnardo's 1999–2000 'Giving Children Back Their Future' campaign.[12]

This was a powerful but very controversial campaign which showed seven babies in adult situations, such as injecting drugs or drinking alcohol, in order to show what the future could be like for children without support. The Committee of Advertising Practice called for the adverts to be banned, observing that they were 'too shocking' to be published. In contrast, Roger Alton of *The Observer* said: 'Anything that wakes people up to this is for the better. People sit around with their heads in the sand too often.'[13]

Ask pupils to consider the following questions:

- ☐ Are the images supportive or manipulative?

- ☐ Are the images or the words more effective, or are they both complementary?

- ☐ Does the end result justify using harrowing images?

---

12 See <http://www.barnardos.org.uk/what_we_do/campaigns/advertising_campaigns/previous_advertising_campaigns/giving_children_back_their_future_advertising_campaign_1999-2000.htm/>.

13 Quoted in BBC, Papers Defy Advert Ban (22 January 2000). Available at: <http://news.bbc.co.uk/1/hi/uk/614319.stm>.

Symbolic images

One way of conveying horror is to use symbolic images. Images of piles of shoes and glasses from Auschwitz are not violent in themselves, but the horror they imply is almost worse than actual violence. Walking around the United States Holocaust Memorial Museum in Washington, you cannot help but be moved by an image at the museum entrance of a huge, smiling security man. Stephen Tyrone Johns had been shot and killed at the Museum in 2009 by a Holocaust denier and white supremacist. The image itself is a positive one – a smiling young man looking straight at the camera – *but* what it represents is shocking beyond belief. It is what it symbolises that makes the photograph so powerful and compelling.

Images such as the rescue of Reshma Begum seventeen days after the collapse of a clothing factory in Bangladesh, in April 2013, showed the horrific conditions in which some people in the developing world live and work. These types of photographs have a positive side – the triumph of the human spirit, the fortitude of the rescuers, raising awareness of factory conditions. However, do these positive factors balance out the visceral images of death, injury, pain and suffering? Footage of the rescue of the Chilean miners, in August 2010, showed hope after disaster. So, do we also need to see positive images to avoid our compassion fatigue?

I took a group of GCSE pupils to Sanctuary Wood, a museum in Belgium with many First World War artefacts, including 3D images of trench warfare and its resulting injuries. Visitors learn about the lives of the soldiers by walking around the 'trenches' and viewing photographs in a room of image viewers. However, one student was vehement that she should not have been allowed to view these images, claiming that no one should be allowed to look at them – she was visibly shaken and very angry. She was angry about the photographs, but not yet old enough to be angry at the atrocities themselves. Photography has the power to move, to shock, to inspire and always to provoke a reaction.

You can't go around kidding yourself that your
photographs in a few papers will change the world.

Don McCullin

Using photography to support SMSC

There are lots of definitions of SMSC – you can unpick the social, moral, spiritual aspects of your curriculum ad infinitum – but the fact remains that you cannot be an outstanding teacher or school without addressing *all* of these aspects. However, just using a tick list – which you can show to Ofsted or other visitors – does not mean that these are fundamental qualities of your work as a teacher.

How can we expect children to develop a proper understanding of society unless we model respect? How can we create a sense of awe and wonder for learning without examining a sense of right and wrong, of making choices, of looking at what stops us in our tracks and makes us catch our breath? How can we expect collaborative and cooperative learning unless we give pupils a chance to work together and encourage them to listen to one another's opinions?

If we keep our pupils' outlook too narrow and focus just on our own school and our local community, we will miss out on so much and run the risk of young people not understanding and empathising with other peoples and cultures. All of the above are common sense: we need our pupils to think and examine their own ideas, beliefs, standards, the world around them and the way in which they interact with others.

You will already have clear ways of ensuring that you foster respect for others via work in tutor groups, assemblies, anti-bullying weeks, peer support systems and many more. Nevertheless, there are two key ways that photography can help in the promotion of clear SMSC values:

1 As a recording tool. Yes, this is so obvious it hardly bears saying, but is this actually happening in your school? Are we taking photographs of those key times when SMSC is evident and then celebrating this? Maybe we do if it's a Comic Relief day or a charity event, but SMSC is about so much more than that. What about the 'little acts' that almost go unnoticed – the child who finds a toy and hands it in, the children who befriend a new pupil to the class, the child who creates a special piece of artwork or music. There may be times during your day, week or lesson when you experience a 'light bulb' moment. People call them different things – 'champagne moments' or even just 'moments' – but these are the special times that make you remember why you became a teacher. Why not find a way to capture these moments and celebrate your comments with a 'Wall of Fame' or a 'Gallery of Specialness'?

The words *spiritual*, *moral*, *social* and *cultural* will be fairly meaningless to many children, so it's important to frame the display in child-friendly language. What about replacing the headings with 'Wow', 'Getting It Right', 'Sharing' and 'Hello World'. Obviously, these are just starting points and pupils can create their own headings for their gallery.

What photographs might go under each heading? If you take the 'Social' heading, for example, you might think about times when pupils are working together, listening and helping each other out.

Create your own headings for an SMSC 'Gallery of Specialness'.

As a class, create ideas for what photographs could go into each section.

Turn these words into word clouds using www.wordle. net or www.tagxedo.com.

Take photographs at the time, if possible, or afterwards of the work the pupils produce or of the pupils themselves and celebrate their achievements, so that the children are proud to appear on the Wall of Fame. It is special to care for others, to be creative, to listen and work together – we encourage all of these things, so why not celebrate them? As well as you taking photographs, leave a camera or an iPad on your desk and encourage pupils to take photographs when they see something that deserves celebrating. These displays should be 'working displays' and not static. By that, I mean that images should be captured immediately, Polaroid-style, printed off and stuck on the wall. Have a stock of sticky notes or fancy cards (obviously made by pupils) at the side of the wall and allow pupils, parents, office staff, governors – anyone – to write positive comments to add to your wall. Then stand back and watch it grow!

Photograph the hands of everyone in the class – or school! Create a border for your wall made from these images.

2 As a prompt for pupils to respond to. If SMSC is to be embedded properly, it needs to be clear in our curriculum. By using images as a stimulus, you create opportunities for discussion and deeper thinking, for reflection and sharing. Choose your images carefully though – this is not about 'oh look at those poor people'; it's about developing an understanding and deepening our questioning in order to allow pupils to have a personal response.

Philosophy for Children is a good tool to use when discussing photographs as it adds structure and leads pupils through a straightforward thinking process. After looking at images and responding, pupils can then start to take their own images that they feel will generate an emotional response. What do they think is special about themselves, their area, their culture? How can they show its differences and similarities in their photographs?

Put a border around your classroom window (or, if you have time, the outline of a camera with the window as the LED screen at the back of the camera). Put the heading 'Today's Photograph' above it. Use this as the basis for discussion and to encourage pupils to *look* at what is happening.

Photography is a way of feeling, of touching, of loving.
What you have caught on film is captured forever …
it remembers the little things, long after you have forgotten everything.

Aaron Siskind

Today everything exists to end in a photograph.
Susan Sontag

Chapter 6

Photography outside of education

Photographs as memories and sentiments

Depending on how old you are, you may remember some of these scenarios:

- Putting your film in a prepaid Truprint or Bonusprint envelope and sending it off to be developed.

- Waiting two weeks for the prints to arrive.

- Ordering an extra set of prints (at half price!) for your aunt/granny/mum.

- Being so disappointed that out of twenty-four photos (you had to be posh to buy films that had thirty-six exposures) only two were in focus – the rest had missing heads and limbs and were blurred beyond recognition.

- Being 'trendy' and buying a black-and-white film.

- Being excited when they brought out the format that allowed one large copy and two miniature copies of your photo on the same print.

- The arrival of high-street developers, like Max Speilmann and Boots, so photographs now took only a week to develop.

- Paying extra (this was really expensive!) for a twenty-four-hour developing service. (Take out a new mortgage and you could have your prints done in an hour!)

All of the above seem laughable now. We have digital cameras which create images that we can see instantaneously. Something that happens across the globe can be on our Internet screens/smart-phones/iPads within minutes. Our hard drives are full of unprinted and unedited photos. It seems unbelievable that we had to wait weeks to see our images. You may have boxes full of packets of photographs from your childhood, but a hard drive full of images from just the last few years. Many people no longer print photographs but share them online via a blog, Facebook, Flickr, Twitter or Instagram.

Does this mean we see our images differently? We still have important photos printed and framed or made into photo books, but usually these are not 'everyday' images. I have data from a few years ago saved on floppy disks – these are obviously now obsolete and everything on them is inaccessible. The typical storage capacity of a floppy disk was 1 or 2 MB. I am currently using a USB external storage device which has the capacity to store 500GB. Technology is advancing so rapidly that new models of computers, storage devices and printers are being developed literally on a daily basis. Meanwhile, 3D printers are currently being developed for home desk-top use. At this rate of development, how long will it be before CDs and USB drives become obsolete? We now store information in 'the cloud' and sync all of our information – but for how long will this be accessible before another system is introduced?

Give pupils a quote about photography or education.[1]

Illustrate this with a suitable image to create a poster.

---

1 For some suggestions visit <http://www.brainyquote.com/>.

The Burning House

If you had to leave your house because of a disaster, be it a flood or a fire, what would you take with you? How many of you would grab a photograph in some form or other? Why are photographs so important? Perhaps it is because they help us to 'freeze' our memories. I have images in my head from my childhood which I'm sure I wasn't old enough to consciously remember. Many of these 'memories' must come from the photographs that I have been shown or have seen displayed for years on the walls of my parents' house.

> **If you could only save one photograph – which one would it be?**

Foster Huntington has set up an amazing blog called The Burning House and followed this up with a book of the same name. In it he asks:

> *If your house was burning, what would you take with you? It's a conflict between what's practical, valuable and sentimental. What you would take reflects your interests, background, and priorities. Think of it as an interview condensed into one question.*[2]

The Burning House evolved from a discussion about personalities for dating site profiles. Huntington posed a question about what individuals would take from a burning house and realised that this actually revealed a great deal about your values and what is important to you. He brought this idea to the Internet – people were invited to upload their own burning house images – where it went viral and resulted in an amazing book, which shows in fascinating clarity what is important to us.

> **What does it mean to 'go viral'? What sort of videos and ideas do this?**
>
> **Find examples and analyse them.**

It is interesting that in a list of the most popular items people would save, photographs came second. For younger people, their photographs tended to be on electronic devices but older people had actual photographs. Others items included letters, postcards, items of clothing, keepsakes, journals, childhood toys and jewellery. Many of the items are of sentimental rather than monetary value.

---

2 F. Huntington, *The Burning House: What Would You Take?* (New York: HarperCollins, 2012), p. ix. See also <http://theburninghouse.com/> or on Twitter @The Burning House.

I created my own burning house image, with each item being important in its own way:

- My childhood teddy bear – it's old and tatty and one ear needs sewing back on properly.

- My Olympus SLR camera – it represents all of my camera equipment.

- The first Mother's Day card that my youngest son (now 24) made for me at nursery.

- My iPhone – it has all of my contacts, numbers, e-mails and loads of photographs – I would be lost if I didn't have the information and images on it.

- An old camera – it doesn't work and the leather cover is damaged, but it belonged to my dad who gave it to me.

- Baby jacket and hat, clock toy and hospital sock – all of which belonged to my eldest son, who died when he was only 8 weeks old.

- Musical toy – again, this belonged to my eldest son. He was in intensive care for eight weeks and this music calmed him down. It still has his hospital tag attached.

- A photograph of myself holding Matthew (my eldest son) with my parents.

- A photograph of my two sons as babies in a frame which stands on my bedside table.

The most important things in my image are irreplaceable and of no monetary value, but that's what makes them so special. Huge parts of my life are revealed here; there are other parts which are equally special but as I still have these people (my wonderful husband and younger son) with me, I could take more images of them and create more memories. I'm sure that by looking at these items you can tell what is important to me.

It is interesting that my photo reveals a lot more about me than would be the case if I were to write a paragraph about myself. If you do this task honestly, you can't avoid revealing what is meaningful to you.

Try creating your own burning house image. What does it reveal about you? You could use this with a new class to develop their questioning skills and also for them to learn a little more about you.

Ideas

- Look at the Burning House blog or book. In pairs, pupils could select a person and their belongings and 'introduce' them to the rest of the group. The class can then use deductive reasoning to decide what they feel is important to their person.

- Foster Huntington began to travel the world asking different people what they would take – who would pupils like to interview? Which six places would they visit to ask different people and get a range of ideas?

- Create 'imaginary' Burning House photographs for characters from different periods in history. Pupils may have to draw or make some of the objects to include in their photograph.

- Create a class Burning House image – what is important in your classroom? Ask other classes in your school to do this too.

- Ask parents to join in – each child could then take an image at home. This could then form the basis for a display/book/video

- Ask the pupils to discuss whether our choice of objects reflects our age, background and values.

Dear Photograph

Another book and blog which work on the idea of the importance of photographs and memories is Dear Photograph by Taylor Jones.[3] According to *Time* magazine:

> *Some of the Web's best sites consist of variations on one simple idea. In the case of Dear Photograph, that idea is taking a snapshot – usually one featuring one or more people and dating from the film-photography era – and holding it up against the original setting so that past and present blend into a new work of art.*[4]

The idea began when Jones realised that he was looking at a photograph in an album of his brother who was 3 at the time, but he was also looking at his brother now sitting in exactly the same place as where the photograph was taken. He held up the photograph and incorporated it into the current scene, adding what his brother would say to the person/image in the photograph – and the idea for Dear Photograph was born. In his introduction to the book, Jones says that he hopes it will 'inspire you to search for those pictures of days gone by and revisit the places of your past'.

The book is an emotional rollercoaster – messages to loved ones no longer alive, messages to children, parents and ancestors. There are memories of houses, schools, special occasions and people, all brought up to date in contemporary settings and often with very poignant messages.

The image above is of my son when he just a toddler. He loved playing in granddad's greenhouse. What might he want to say to his younger self? What might I want to say to his younger self, looking back and knowing what we know now about how his life has turned out?

---

3 T. Jones, *Dear Photograph* (New York: HarperCollins, 2012) or visit <http://dearphotograph.com/>.

4 Time, 50 Websites That Make the Web Great (16 August 2011). Available at: <http://content.time.com/time/specials/packages/article/0,28804,2087815_2087868_2087873,00.html>.

Ideas

- Ask parents, grandparents, staff or the local community for copies of images of your school and local area that could be used in a Dear Photograph project.

- Where would you take the new photograph?

- What does the old photograph show you about any changes that have taken place?

- What messages do you want to 'send' to the people in the photograph?

- Involve parents – can pupils create a Dear Photograph at home?

- Look at the book and website – read and enjoy!

- Choose three images from the website that you think are special and explain why.

Operation Photo Rescue

Over the last few years, there have been a number of tragic natural disasters ranging from tsunamis and hurricanes to earthquakes and floods. The cost to society in physical and mental terms is staggering: loss of life, damage to property, whole communities ripped apart .The images of grief and devastation seen by the world through photographs and news reports are etched in our minds.

However, humans are resilient and communities pull together to rebuild their lives. Practical issues are tackled first – housing, physical well-being and safety. As in Maslow's hierarchy of needs, biological and physiological needs must be met first.

But some things are irreplaceable. Earlier in this chapter we saw that in a danger situation, such as burning house scenarios, many people would save photos or photo albums. These are the items that cannot be replaced. The smiling toddler in the damaged image is now a gangly teenager or an adult, so the image can't possibly be retaken. We have a mental image, but often that isn't is enough.

Following Hurricane Katrina, an organisation called Operation Photo Rescue was set up by Dave Ellis and Becky Self in order to aid people whose photographs have been damaged or destroyed.[5] It is a non-profit organisation which now has over 2,000 volunteers worldwide. But these are not the same as your 'traditional' volunteers following a disaster. They are more concerned with preserving memories than rebuilding houses. They understand that emotional well-being is as important as physical well-being. The strap line on their website says 'Insurance doesn't restore memories … but we do'.

Operation Photo Rescue operates in areas following natural disasters and, with a lot of support from various individuals and organisations, they set up drop-in centres where people can take up to twenty damaged photographs to be restored free of charge. These are digitally photographed and then sent to volunteer photographers and restoration experts across the globe. Over 9,000 images have currently been

5 See <http://www.operationphotorescue.org/>.

restored. As one person who has benefitted from the service says on the website, Operation Photo Rescue 'can take another person's memories and rebuild them a micro inch at a time to make a picture whole again'.

Ideas

- Operation Photo Rescue produces an information sheet about how to restore damaged photographs. As part of a science lesson, explore conditions that have an effect on photographs, such as damp, mould, condensation, water and smoke.

- Mantle of the Expert is a great way for pupils to be 'in the moment' and to understand events and feelings.[6] The idea of a photo restoration company lends itself to this kind of dramatic working. What sort of roles would there be in this company (e.g. press officers, scientists, Photoshop experts, counsellors)? What would be your way in to the task – perhaps a bundle of damaged photos or a woman sitting on her own with a crumpled photograph in her hand?

- What makes a photograph valuable? A square of 6 x 4 photographic paper has very little intrinsic value, so what is it that makes it so precious?

---

6 See <http://www.mantleoftheexpert.com/>.

> Ask for images from the local community and organise a historical exhibition of your area.
>
> Take these shots again so that you can compare then and now.

- Individuals are allowed to take up to twenty photographs to be restored by Operation Photo Rescue. If you could only choose twenty images (these can be descriptions of mental images – they do not have to be actual photographs) what would they be? This would make a good homework task to be discussed at home.

- The children could research natural disasters over the last ten years and, using Creative Commons images (see Chapter 1), search for iconic photographs from these events. Choose an image that pupils feel best represents this disaster and then place this image on the appropriate place on a world map. This could then lead to discussions about the links between the types of disaster that occur and their location. By using the images they have found, pupils can begin to look at the human elements of these disaster stories and how they affect the lives of people in those areas.

- Research methods of restoring images – then have a go!

What I like about photographs is that they capture a moment …
that's gone forever, impossible to reproduce.

Karl Largerfeld

Sutcliffe Gallery

Every Now and Then is a book of original images of Whitby by Frank Sutcliffe, taken in the late nineteenth century, which have been placed alongside their modern equivalent, taken by Michael J. Shaw.[7] The book provides a great stimulus for historical study, but it can also be used as a model or template for pupils to create their own book which takes old images and recreates them.

100 Cameras

100 cameras is a project that was started by four women in New York.[8] The idea is a simple one: you give a child a camera, the child takes photographs, you sell the photograph on behalf of the child – the money then supports that child's community.

The images on the website are stunning and show communities through the eyes of their children. You can also adopt a camera or donate to the project.

It is worth investigating this site for the stunning photographs the children have produced and the insight the images give into different ways of life, but also for how photography can be used in a positive and supportive way as a tool for change.

> See the calendar challenge in Chapter 10 and use it as a starting point for using photography to raise money for charity.

---

7   M. J. Shaw and F. M. Sutcliffe, *Every Now and Then* (Whitby: Sutcliffe Gallery, 2002).

8   See <http://www.100cameras.org/>.

Part II

Projects and applications

When words become unclear,
I shall focus with photographs.
When images become inadequate,
I shall be content with silence.
Ansel Adams

Chapter 7

Visual literacy

We live in a world which is increasingly visual. The vast majority of us own a mobile phone which has the facility to take photographs, then edit and upload these at the touch of a button. We can access the Internet, watch live news, get up-to-the-minute images of events from across the globe, and yet we take all of this for granted. Just a hundred years ago, it would have taken several days for news of disasters to reach us, yet we now get our news almost instantaneously. Many of the large photography agencies can have images online within minutes of an event, and we can all join in the debate and upload images via social media sites such as Facebook and Twitter.

What is visual literacy?

The term 'visual literacy' was first coined by the writer John Debes in 1968,[1] and refers to our 'ability to construct meaning from visual images'.[2] In the same way that pupils need to be numerate and literate, it is important that, as we live in an ever more visual world, they can interpret and read images. Can they detect manipulation and bias, as well as looking for the clues within the images themselves? Visual literacy involves being able to read photographs with reference to social and cultural contexts. It is about looking for the meaning and inference within images and going beyond the obvious. Being visually literate allows pupils to understand the difference between technique and aesthetics and enables them to form their own opinions about images based on clear analysis and evaluation skills.

---

1 J. Debes, Some Foundations for Visual Literacy, *Audiovisual Instruction* 13 (1968): 961–964.
2 C. Giorgis, N. J. Johnson, A. Bonomo, C. Colbert, A. Conner and G. Kauffman, Visual Literacy, *Reading Teacher* 53(2) (1999): 146–153.

Research has shown that a child as young as 12 months can equate a picture of an object with the object itself. We teach children to read using picture books – employing images as the basis of conversation and description. The understanding of the written word doesn't come until much later in a child's development. As Anne Bamford observes: 'Understanding pictures is a vital life enriching necessity. Not to understand them is visual illiteracy.'[3]

Iconic images

Images stay in our mind and we can often visualise events even if we can't remember dates and facts. How many of the events below can you picture and actually describe?

- ☐ Tiananmen Square protests of 1989. (How many tanks are there? Are they in a horizontal line or behind one another?)

- ☐ Martin Luther King's 1963 'I Have a Dream' speech. (Is this image colour or black and white?).

- ☐ Hiroshima bomb. (What shape is the 'cloud'?)

- ☐ Nelson Mandela's release from prison in 1990. (Who is with him in this photograph?)

- ☐ The 1989 fall of the Berlin Wall. (What are the people in the photograph doing?)

What other images would you say were 'iconic'? (Take a look at Brad Finger's *50 Photos You Should Know* and *13 Photos Children Should Know* for some ideas.[4])

---

3   A. Bamford, Visual Literacy White Paper (2003). Available at: <http://wwwimages.adobe.com/www.adobe.com/content/dam/ Adobe/en/education/pdfs/visual-literacy-wp.pdf>.

4   B. Finger, *50 Photos You Should Know* (London: Prestel, 2012) and *13 Photos Children Should Know* (London: Prestel, 2011).

SIFT

In order to have a structure for 'looking' at photographs and trying to read them, you can use the acronym SIFT.

See

Infer

Feel

Technique

= SIFT

To test how this works in practice, we are going to 'sift' out what is important in the photograph opposite of St Pancras station, in London.

Before using SIFT as a frame, you could simply get pupils to write their response to the image without any help. You could then compare this with using SIFT to see if it does help to clarify their thoughts.

See

This means literally 'say what you see'. It can be done as a discussion or the children can write their thoughts and ideas onto large sheets of paper, sticky notes or note apps on their iPads – whichever is your preferred method. Here are some examples:

People, escalator, shops, arches, coloured rings, clock (8.20), people sitting on benches, suit-cases, notice boards, a domed metal ceiling with glass, arched windows, a plant, lights, a bar, red-brick walls, two levels, bright clothing

It is not necessary to 'over-think' this stage. You are not yet asking pupils to say what is important in the image – all they are doing here is looking closely and writing down everything they see.

Infer

At the infer stage we are considering what we can infer or deduce from the image. Do any of our words or ideas from what we can see give us any additional information about the image?

- Are there any clues as to the date of the photograph – is it modern or historical?

- Is there anything which tells us where or what the photograph is showing?

- Do we know what time of day it is? Is that important or not?

- Can we tell which country this is set in? Is it a rich or a poor place?

- Why might this photograph have been taken? What could be the purpose? Who could be the intended audience?

- Is there anything to suggest that this is not an authentic image or that it has been manipulated?

Obviously, as adults (and as I've told you exactly where the image was taken), we know that this is a contemporary image set in a large train station. But how would you use the clues in the image to back up what you can infer from the image itself? The Olympic rings, for example, date this, as does the style of clothing and bags.

If you get a magnifying glass, you can see that the words 'underground' and 'St Pancras' are visible – they are blurred but readable. Encourage pupils to become detective-like and really try to look at the photograph as if it were a piece of evidence.

Feel

The feeling part of this analysis is more subjective, so the photographs will elicit different responses from different individuals. This isn't a controversial image so it should not provoke any extreme reactions, but pupils can still say what feelings it evokes in them.

- The feeling of the photograph (but remember this is subjective and so merely my opinion) can be summed up by the words 'busy' and 'movement'. It feels bright, light and positive.

- The feeling that this image evokes could be anticipation – you may love travelling and this photograph could remind you of the excitement at the start of a journey. For others, it could be worry as they don't like busy places and get anxious about travelling.

Technique

The aspects that you could look at are:

- Composition – include angle and vantage point, rule of thirds, leading lines, symmetry, perspective, format (landscape or portrait)

- Focal point/focus

- Depth of focus

- Colour – is the image in colour, black and white or sepia?

- Shutter speed – movement or frozen action

- Any Photoshop work or image manipulation

- Exposure/use of light

Once they have worked through the SIFT process, ask the pupils to compare their analysis of the image prior to using SIFT and then either re-write or re-discuss their original response to the image. Hopefully they will have deepened their understanding.

See Chapter 1: Camera basics

Getting inside an image

One way of using photographs is to get pupils to imagine that they are actually inside it – part of the image itself. You could use an image as a stimulus for writing and storytelling, such as the one of St Pancras station on page 109. Ask students to recreate the scene of a busy railway station in the classroom using the image as a guide. What are people doing? Are they in groups? Who are they with? Are they carrying cases or bags? Where are they going? Where have they come from? Are they happy (e.g. going to meet family after working away)? Are they sad (have they just said goodbye to a partner for several months – why is that?)? Are they worried (are they on their way to a job interview after being made redundant months ago?)? This part of the process relies on storytelling techniques as well as using their imaginations and actually turning the characters in the photograph into real people with real stories.

You could do some practical work to complement this. For example, where can you travel to from St Pancras? Which countries does Eurostar go to? Look at the image – the Olympic rings are visible – so what people might be around who wouldn't normally be there? What is security like at train stations? What retail shops and restaurants are there?

If you are going to suggest that pupils recreate this image, a good way of getting them to be 'in character' is to ask them to create a freeze-frame. When you tap them on the shoulder, they should unfreeze and say one sentence about who they are or what they are thinking. Use the image faithfully – for instance, the pupils couldn't say, 'I'm on my way home as it's Christmas', because there is no evidence of it being that time of year. This helps us to get a real feel for a photograph and allows pupils to show empathy and yet be creative.

Fill in the image

Ben Heine has created a thought-provoking but humorous series of works called Pencil vs Camera.[5] He takes images but adds his own ideas about what is happening within the photograph as a hand holding a torn piece of paper containing a pencil sketch.

Pupils can create their own images in this style using tracing paper and their imagination. There is also an app called Ripped which allows you to turn part of your photograph into a sketch similar to Heine's. The app allows you to use presets for the 'ripped' section or draw your own. Pupils could also replace the sketched part with a drawing of their own.

© Ben Heine 2013 – benheine.com.

Sheffield city centre – Ripped.

5   See <http://www.flickr.com/photos/benheine/sets/72157623723956821/>.

Six words – one photograph

Ernest Hemmingway is credited with the story: 'For sale: baby shoes, never worn.' Legend has it that this was in response to a bet to write a six-word story that could make people cry. Whether he actually did write this is not relevant here; what is important is the brevity of narrative used to sum up a whole story.

This is an exercise that works well with pupils of all ages, although it is a good idea to model this with pupils as a whole-class exercise first.

Use the image overleaf (or any photograph of barbed wire) as an example.

Ask pupils to work in groups and generate words from this image using the SIFT technique described above. Begin with 'concrete' words (i.e. what can they *see*), for example:

Sky, blue, barbed wire, spikes, curls, clouds

Next, what can we *infer* from this image? This isn't meant to generate words but to help us understand the context. For example:

That it is a dangerous situation. We are stopping something or someone either getting in or getting out. There is tension here. Is it to protect or limit?

Then ask the children to think of words that describe their *feelings* about the image or other situations that it may remind them of. Examples might include:

Freedom, harm, pain, escape, confined, prisoner, sad, scared, barbs, fear, hope, alone, no entry

The next stage is to consider where this photo could be. Who is looking at it? Who is narrating the story? It is important to stress that there are no wrong answers.

The children's responses can be written on sticky notes or pieces of paper and physically moved around to see what stories emerge. Alternatively, place the words on pieces of paper around the room so pupils can select their six words after walking round and considering a whole range of ideas that have been generated collectively.

Then ask them to write their six-word stories. Here are some examples:

Barred entry, alone. Blue sky blocked.

Confined, imprisoned, no escape, no hope.

Freedom barred, no hope of escape.

If we are told something about the context of an image, does this alter our viewpoint? In fact, the barbed wire in this image was on top of an amusement arcade in Cleethorpes! Does this change our view of the story?

Vandals again, barbed wire – no thefts!

Ideas

- Give the image to the whole class but only tell half of them where it was taken.

- Ask pupils to compare their stories.

- How much are we influenced by what other people tell us about images and stories?

- How much do we infer from images?

> Take a series of photographs of either shadows or silhouettes.

The six-word stories below are examples from a Year 6 class at Shafton Primary School, in Barnsley. They were inspired by the image to the left of a light show taken at a local stately home.

Villagers startled and amazed by vision.
Drawn as moths to a flame.
Bright light quickens the villagers' heartbeats.
Bright light quickens the villagers' footsteps
In a lightening flash, all was revealed.

This image could be used as part of a modelling exercise, in which you work through the six-word story process with the pupils before they have a go at the task themselves.

In order to extend this task, ask pupils to create an image which could be used as the basis for a six-word story. Your discussion of guidelines could include the following points:

- It is important to include some element of mystery or ambiguity – how could you do this?

- Take your image from an unusual angle so that the viewer has to really think about what they are looking at.

- Only include part of your subject – the section that is missing could lead to uncertainty and questions.

- Think about ambiguity of setting – for example, place an object somewhere you would not expect to find it.

- Look at the background of your image – is it distracting, or does it add to the image?

- Use everyday objects photographed in an unusual or abstract way.

Another option would be to start with the same light-show image, but edit it in various ways. Give a different edit of the same photo to different groups. Does this make a difference to the stories the children produce? Does colour help determine the mood of the image? Do they automatically assume one image is older than another? Does a black-and-white image make them look at the subject matter in a different way? Can they be manipulated into looking at an image in a certain way?

Work in pairs – take six images of your choice *but* one of you must work in black and white and one in colour. Compare your images.

This giraffe can be found in the Winter Garden Gallery in Sheffield. It fits with the criteria outlined above as it is unusual and it is made from everyday objects (cutlery), but these have been formed into a giraffe. There are no background distractions and, as an image, it is open to a range of interpretations.

A Year 6 class examined the photograph to the left and their six-word responses included:

- *Literal*:
  Lots of scrap creates a masterpiece.
  It's modern, it's new, it's scrap.

- *Contextual*:
  Cutlery creature lives in steel city.
  Cutting edge creature sparks steel city.

- *Thoughtful*:
  Golden treasures can be found within.

- *Humorous*:
  Artist, no cutlery, starves to death.
  Mum mystified by empty cutlery drawer.

Experiment – find a way to take photographs of everyday objects using a magnifying glass or a microscope.

100 Word Challenge

The 100 Word Challenge is a weekly writing challenge organised by Julia Skinner via Twitter (@theheadsoffice).[6] Children are encouraged to write a creative piece that is 100 words long, prompted by phrases or images. What makes this special is that they are given an audience for their work via the website. Once published on their school blog, the teacher can link the stories to the 100WC site, and a member of the 100 Word Challenge team (teachers or supportive adults) will make constructive comments. Teachers can also read and comment on the work of other children, so there is a real sense of sharing and pride. The 100WC team then recommend pieces of writing to be commended in the weekly showcase.

You can browse the website and share writing with your pupils, join in or use the idea in-house.

To kick off the project with your pupils, select a striking image as a stimulus and ask them to write 100 words on it. Try it with the boots image opposite.

This image was used as the prompt for a 100-word challenge. (You can find hundreds of other examples on the 100 Word Challenge website.) The stories that were created were incredibly varied and creative. Opening sentences such as, 'Everybody said I was crazy. They said the floods were a dangerous thing and were not to be misunderstood …' and 'As the boots waited for their new victim …'

are clear examples of the imaginative writing that was produced. One beautiful piece of work by a Year 3 pupil, Troy, even told the story (here unedited) from the point of view of the puddle:

Another rainy day. I'm getting kicked again and jumped in again. I'm FURIOUS and ANGRY. I'm going to get my own back because they don't know that a puddle can have feelings. So, when the man who always walks his dog by, I sucked him in. Now, that is proper revenge through all them gnarled, wrinkly and old leaves … never seen again … By the way he was DELICIOUS, also my puddle is enormous it goes right down to the ground where lots of mud all slushy and splashy … though his dog got away because he was scared.

See Chapter 1: Creative Commons Images

---

6 See <http://www.100wc.net/>.

Images as a stimulus for investigation

The two images to the right show children in Uganda playing with their toys.

These photographs are examples of how you can use images as a starting point for further investigation. (Remind the children to use SIFT when reading photographs.)

- Take photographs of the games children play today and compare them with games from previous generations.

- Undertake research by having discussions with grandparents or find out about toys in the past. Many local museums have excellent toy sections (but be prepared to be dismayed when you see the toys that you owned in the history section!).

- What was the game Ring a Ring o' Roses associated with?

- Write a clear set of illustrated instructions for someone who has never played hopscotch before.

- Find out about Gabriele Galimberti's Toy Stories.[7]

- What game do you think the children in the photographs are playing? What are their toys made from? Why are their toys made from these materials? Why can't they just buy toys? Discussion prompts could be: would only having one toy make it more special? Are toys a necessity to child development or a luxury?

- Are handmade toys more meaningful than bought ones? Do/did you have a favourite toy? What made it special?

- Design a game which can be played with a 'toy' like the ones being played with by the children in the images to the right – include an instruction leaflet.

- Develop a new toy using only scrap materials. Create the toy, packaging and instructions in order to pitch to a toy company. Consider why this is a good idea and how the toy will be used. (You could set this up as a *Dragons' Den*-style pitch.)

7 See <http://www.gabrielegalimberti.com/> and page 192.

A photograph is usually looked at – seldom looked into.

Ansel Adams

When we use images as our stimulus or source, they can tell us a great deal about the era in which the photograph was taken. For example, if we examine the photographs of Lewis Hines, we can see exactly what the life was like for children in the early 1900s in the United States. His photography represents a form of social documentary, but it was the fact that he based his images on what was 'the norm' – the everyday and the mundane – that gives us most insight.

Most of us tend to photograph what is special – an amazing or one-off event. In doing so, we have a good insight into life today, but only one aspect of it. I'm sure that there were millions of photographs taken of the 2012 Olympics or the Queen's Golden Jubilee street parties, but what about that same street on a normal Monday morning? Instead of sporting events, what about the inside of a supermarket or a fast-food outlet? We are fascinated by images of American diners from the 1940s and 1950s so, by the same logic, children in the future may also learn from our mundane moments.

Ask pupils to create a 'Mundane Memories' board – what would they take photographs of to represent a visual record of their everyday lives? By photographing the commonplace and putting these together, they will be creating a special historical record for the future.

To photograph the mundane today is to create the historical source of the future.

Jane Hewitt

Chapter 8

Street art

The art of discovery

The longer you teach, the further away you are from your own school days – that's obvious. What isn't so immediately obvious is the fact that the longer you teach, the more you realise how much you don't know and how much you still have to learn.

I found myself being really excited about learning something new recently. It happened, as a lot of good learning does, by accident. I realised that I was being hooked in and as soon as I began to make connections, I wanted to know more and began to research, plan visits and ask questions.

I often plan days out with my camera, usually with a clear aim in mind as to what I'm looking for, but on this occasion I was helping out a friend's son who is an architecture student. He wanted to look at the juxtaposition of old and new buildings, so we headed to Kelham Island, in Sheffield. This is one of the city's oldest industrial districts – a 900-year-old manmade island – where abandoned factories sit alongside trendy cafes, modern apartments and a museum.

We wandered happily for an hour or so and then literally stumbled across the image opposite of a monster pulling a ship on the rear wall of a pub.

It was fascinating – so much detail, so unexpected and so clever! We couldn't see any tag or labels, and immediately we were hooked. The questions came naturally: who painted it? Who could we ask

about it? Who did it 'belong' to? Did it represent something? Who was the 'man' at the front? What was the 'story'? Again, we were intrigued but there was nothing to give us any information about the artist.

On returning home, I edited my photographs and posted them on my blog and on the SWOP blog.[1] I did think about asking permission to use the images but I wasn't sure who they 'belonged' to – thus opening up the debate surrounding street art and private property.

See Chapter 1: Camera basics	See Chapter 7: Visual literacy
Copyright	Six words – one photo

Throughout the history of street art, the question is constantly being asked as to whether it is vandalism or art. In many cases, what was once seen as destructive and criminal is now being commissioned by local councils and advertising companies. Sheffield has recently seen a new piece of street art by Fauna Graphic, which commemorates 100 years since the development of stainless steel by Harry Brearley.[2] This can be seen on Howard Street, just across from the train station and its construction was made into a time-lapse movie by Richard Bolam.[3]

1 See <http://sixwordsonephoto.blogspot.co.uk/>.
2 See <http://www.faunagraphic.co.uk/>.
3 R. Bolam, 100 Years of Stainless Steel: Faunagraphic Mural of Harry Brearley [video] (2013). Available at: <https://vimeo.com/65722308>.

Fauna Graphic has produced a superb example of street art, which combines a whole range of ideas that children could pursue:

- Local history/interest – Harry Brearley was born in Sheffield and is the inventor of stainless steel.

- Science – why doesn't stainless steel rust?

- Maths – the use of grids to scale up the image.

- Art – the design and application (the mural was painted using mainly spray paint).

- Use of video and apps – time-lapse photography as a historical record.

Why does street art figure so prominently in a book about photography? Well, sometimes the only way of preserving these art works is to photograph them. The space available for street art is often limited and so work is sometimes painted over, as in the skateboard area of the South Bank in London.

Image of Harry Brearley by Fauna Graphic Pinhole style, inset image – preparations and drawing to scale using a grid.

In many cases, street art is created on the walls of derelict buildings or areas of urban decay, so it is not readily accessible to the general public. There have been recent instances of street art being chipped off walls to 'frame' or sell it on, particularly if they were believed to be by a famous artist, such as Banksy.

Similarly, the work of 3D pavement chalk artists, such as Julian Beever,[4] can be superb and create stunning optical illusions based on perspective, but, by virtue of the medium used, the work is transitory. Photography then is a tool to help us record and create history.

We can all look at a piece of street art, or a photograph of the work, and see something very different to the next person. Our perception depends on our preconceived ideas, on our knowledge of what we are seeing, on our openness to the idea of the work and of the work itself. The quote by Henry Thoreau, 'It's not what you look at that matters, it's what you see', reinforces this idea. Can we see beauty in something that others regard as vandalism? There is the most insightful comment in Gary Shove's book, *Untitled III: This is Street Art*: 'Thinking (understanding) and vision (perception) are the total responsibility of the reader.'[5]

Obviously, as a teacher and a responsible citizen, you are not going to encourage your pupils to head to the nearest railway line and begin a graffiti artwork project! But you could turn this into a learning exercise which requires negotiating skills, organisation and creativity. For example, find a wall or an area in the school that has potential to be a legitimate mural or piece of street art. Then ask the pupils to consider:

- Who can give us permission to use the wall (there are opportunities for discussion about the concept of property – is street art owned by the artist, the owner of the wall, the council?) – in practical terms, who do we need to write to or contact for permission?

- Prepare a letter or a 'pitch' for your proposed project.

- Do we want to contact an artist who is skilled in this kind of work? Which artists might we consider? How do we make contact?

- What do we want our street art to look like? Content and message are important here as well as ideas around style and colour.

- How will we finance this artwork?

- We are creating a piece of history, so we will want to photograph and record the process and the end result. What methods will we use, both in recording and presenting our work?

It is worth drawing your attention to the language used above – 'us' and 'we'. It is *our* project. This is not a teacher-led process – the teacher and pupils are working as a team and decisions are made jointly.

Use a graffiti style app, such as Graffiti Me, to turn your photographs into graffiti-style artwork. Download a graffiti font to complement your work.

---

4   J. Beever, *Pavement Chalk Artist: The Three Dimensional Drawings of Julian Beever* (New York: Firefly Books, 2010).

5   G. Shove (ed.), *Untitled III: This is Street Art* (Darlington: Carpet Bombing Culture, 2010), Disclaimer II.

To return to the ideas earlier in this chapter about being hooked into learning, a few weeks later I returned to Sheffield city centre to take an image of a *Big Issue* seller for another publication, but decided to walk around and see what else of interest might be around. I was so excited to walk past the artwork to the left on the side of a house just outside the city centre.

It was obvious by the style of the work and the 'main character' that this artwork was by the same person whose work I had seen at Kelham Island. That was it! I was captivated and real research followed! I had a purpose and wanted to find out more about the artist. And it's amazing what you can find if you put your mind to it (what did we do before Google and the Internet?)!

Even if you take an image at face value, there is still amazing scope for children to use their imagination and create stories and whole worlds around these images. If you want to use them just as artwork, there is a great deal that can be developed around technique and style. What about the mathematics of scale? When painting on such huge canvases, how do we go about creating a scale drawing?

I discovered that these works were by a comic book creator and street artist who goes by the name of Phlegm. He is Sheffield based but has other work both locally and much further afield. I found whole groups dedicated to his work on Flickr, articles and interviews, a Google Maps street view walking tour of some of his work, the artist's blog[6] (which contains some amazing sketches which have now been published as a book[7]) and time-lapse videos of his installations.

6   See <http://phlegmcomicnews.blogspot.co.uk/>.
7   See <http://phlegm.bigcartel.com/product/phlegm-book>.

By now, I was completely intrigued by Phlegm and willing to keep delving. Why? Because I wanted to learn and because I was interested. I had to work hard to find what I was looking for, but there was a sense of satisfaction when I did. It was like a journey of discovery – almost like hide and seek!

I even managed to e-mail him to ask for permission to use these images and request a quote. He kindly agreed for the images to be used but said: 'I'm not very good with quotes though to be honest. I prefer to just stick to pictures and keep my trap shut. Peace out – Phlegm.' I think there could be a lesson there!

Below is an installation from March 2013 on the windows of the Millennium Gallery in Sheffield. I simply stumbled across this as I use the gallery grounds as a shortcut from the city centre to the train station.

I'm not very good with quotes to be honest.
I prefer to stick to pictures and keep my trap shut.
Peace out x Phlegm x

Learning about my learning

The whole experience of finding these street art images by Phlegm, and becoming hooked, led me to thinking about how I had enjoyed learning, to examine what had motivated me and to see if this had any parallels to the learning which takes place on a daily basis in the classroom.

- I 'stumbled across' something that I was interested in – no one told me what to research or study.

- I could see real value in the work I was looking it – it was clever and had skill.

- It wasn't easy to find out information – I had to work at it.

- The images raised more questions than they gave answers – in fact, they didn't give any answers!

- I wasn't the only person researching Phlegm's work – I found others who were asking the same questions and we began to share and help one another.

- When I began to have success in my research, it spurred me on to find out more.

- There was a sense of satisfaction in putting pieces of a jigsaw together.

- I now feel that I understand more about street art than when I began learning about it.

All of the above points are obvious, but it was only when I began to unpick my learning that I could see key pointers about motivation and sense of purpose being essential to rich learning. I enjoyed it, I wanted to do it and so I was motivated. The hook for me was my interest being captured by the unknown and proving to myself that I could learn more.

Here are some suggestions for questions you could raise if you used these images in a classroom setting:

- Technical questions about style, medium, perspective, scale, etc.

- Creative questions – who are the characters? Where do they 'live'? What is in the boxes/houses in the ship and monster image (on page 126)? Who or what are the non-human creatures?

- Practical questions – did Phlegm need permission? Who owns the walls? Would there have been any practical issues (e.g. painting on a riverbank)? Did painting in derelict factories involve trespass? How safe is painting on walls, using ladders, in urban spaces?

- Inspirational questions – who influenced Phlegm? What is his background? Where does his inspiration come from?

■ Personal questions – what is the response of individual pupils to both the style of the work and where it is created? If they like the work, which is their favourite installation?

> Take six photographs of different textures around school and create a collage.

Phlegm is a Sheffield-based street artist, which is near where I live, but that's not to say there aren't 'mysteries' in your area which could be explored. It doesn't have to be street paintings – think about other ideas:

■ Architecture – which period is it from? Are there stories behind certain buildings/streets? These don't have to be 'famous' buildings – it could be a faded sign, a broken winch or hook on the side of a building. The image below is of some very faded writing saying 'To the shelter' could be anywhere. As adults, we can hazard a guess when it is from, but to pupils this could be an exciting starting point to the history of their area.

■ You may live near a canal – if so, look at the artwork on boats, the names of boats and old signage.

■ Local factories and industrial development – are there factories which are no longer operational or brand new developments taking place in your area?

■ Local theatres and the interiors of historical buildings. There is a movement of photographers in the UK called Urban Exploration who take images of urban dereliction. Whilst it isn't safe for pupils to visit areas like these themselves, the images are amazing! There are many examples in W. G. Romany's book *Beauty in Decay*[8] and on websites such as www.ukurbex.co.uk.

■ Give pupils old images from around your area – what are these parts of town like now and what has changed?

■ Take photographs of graffiti and ask the children to consider whether this is this art or vandalism. Find images of 'accepted' street art and put these next to your photographs – are they both art or both vandalism? Who decides?

---

8 W. G. Romany, *Beauty in Decay: The Art of Urban Exploration* (Darlington: Carpet Bombing Culture, 2011).

London's South Bank Skatepark

Some areas of street art are now seen as iconic places and none more so, in the UK, than the skateboard park on London's South Bank. It is a world-famous site and has appeared in many films and magazines – it is a great draw for tourists and there are always hordes of photographers snapping the skaters. It is, however, currently under threat of relocation due to refurbishment plans. The public response to this is worth investigating, as it will allow the pupils to look at the value of street art and the reaction to it from different sectors of society.

Using a large sheet of MDF, paper roll or a flat sheet and create some street art on the wall in your classroom. How will you document this?

Use the app iLapse (or any time-lapse app) to create a time-lapse movie of your street art being created.

Chapter 9

Little people

Who are the little people?

The world of the 'little people' is fascinating because it only comes alive when you create it! The figures themselves are actually intended for model railways and are approximately 1 cm high. You can purchase them online – you just need to search for 'Preiser figures'.

These come in different sizes, so it is important to order figures which are 1:87 in scale (the others are too tiny to work with). You can purchase completed figures or plain figures to paint or adapt as you wish.

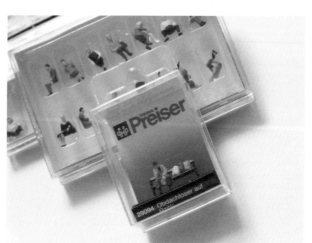

They vary in price from £4 for an individual figure with props to about £10 for a set of decorators or climbers.

A note of caution: not all of the figures are suitable for use in the classroom (e.g. topless sunbathers). Also, some of the images in the books described below are not age appropriate for younger classes (e.g. flashers and prostitutes) but may be suitable as material for discussion with older groups.

JMHewitt

The camera is an instrument that teaches
people how to see without a camera.

Dorothea Lange

Small-scale street art

In order to gain an idea of how these 'little people' can be photographed, have a look at *Little People in the City: The Street Art of Slinkachu*.[1] His work is fascinating and very clever, if a little macabre at times. He creates 'miniature dramas' on city streets and then photographs his work – these are the key record of his creations. He then leaves the scenes on the street for people to find.

In an interview with *The Guardian* in 2009, Slinkachu explains: 'There is a high chance that my installations may never be found. My scenes are made with tiny models and left hidden away on city streets, so they may be lost. But that's what I like about them.'[2] The figures are cleverly integrated into their surroundings and everyday objects are incorporated: two workmen are carrying a Wotsit as if it's a girder or heavy object; a lifeboat is floating in what looks like a lake but is in fact a puddle.

Many of his dramas look as if they are making a statement about society today – such as the use of litter, figures being attacked by giant flies, muggings, young characters wearing hoodies and so on.

There are no explanations, just titles to each piece of work. *Pinned Down* shows a 'little person' fastened to the ground by a safety pin and covered in blood. You could use this as a discussion starter: is it metaphorical? The main point is that a lot of his art relies on the viewer's interpretation.

There was a debate in the media a few years ago as to whether the work produced by artists such as Slinkachu is art at all. You decide – but it is thought-provoking. With regard to the lack of explanation, less is definitely more in some cases! Even if you don't like Slinkachu's work, you might still appreciate the skill and imagination that has gone into it. If it has made you think and created a reaction, surely that is what art should do?

---

1 Slinkachu, *Little People in the City: The Street Art of Slinkachu* (London: Boxtree, 2008).

2 Slinkachu and M. Jenkins, Little Wonders, *The Guardian* (4 April 2009). Available at: <http://www.theguardian.com/travel/2009/apr/04/slinkachu-street-art-graffiti-britain>.

How can we translate 'little people' art for the classroom setting? First, you could introduce images from the growing number of artists and photographers who are working with 'little people'. There are hundreds of images and YouTube videos available online which you could put into a slideshow or print off. As well as Slinkachu, you could consider the following artists:

- Christopher Boffoli, who produces photographs of little people using food as their environment.[3]

- Audrey Heller – there are a range of images on her Facebook page or you can find images by using a search engine.[4]

- Isaac Cordal creates his figures from cement – these feature in his Cement Eclipses project.[5]

If you've ordered some of these figures, place a couple around the room but don't draw attention to them – it is highly unlikely that the pupils will notice them at first. After you have shown them some 'little people' artwork and/or when you draw their attention to them, you will certainly get a 'light bulb moment' or a collective gasp when pupils appreciate quite how small these figures actually are (to gain some idea of the scale, the paper clips in the image below are normal size). They will then be hooked and clamouring to hold them and have a closer look.

The figures themselves are secondary to the creativity that they unleash in pupils. If we are going to create worlds for them to inhabit as the focus of our photography, we need to think about backdrop for the images.

See Chapter 1:
Camera basics

Composition

Use of aperture or macro settings

See Chapter 3: Camera obscuras and pinhole cameras

---

3 See <http://bigappetites.net>.
4 See <https://www.facebook.com/audreyhellerfan>.
5 See <http://www.isaac.alg-a.org/>.

Creating miniature worlds

As the figures are so tiny, they can be positioned with everyday objects to give a surreal feel to photographs – like these miniature painters with a tulip (far right). By thinking carefully about backgrounds, you can emphasise the difference in scale.

Pupils are really creative when given the freedom. The photograph to the right was created by using a pine cone and a Sherbet Dip Dab! Pupils worked out that by using sherbet for snow and pine cones for the trees, they could create a realistic winter scene.

You can experiment using Plasticine, Fimo, modelling clay or homemade salt dough (it's very messy and goes off quickly, but can be made simply and cheaply with salt, flour and water). Create your own props – such as chairs, rocks, trees or even whole scenes. You can take toy cars and smash them up to create crime scenes or make use of everyday objects, such as biscuits, cameras, tea cups – anything! Use sand for roads, pull flowers to pieces, use food or toys – the only limit is your imagination! Just allow pupils to play and be creative.

Here is a list of some of the issues you may wish to consider:

- Scale is important – in order to introduce a sense of their actual size, we need to incorporate recognisable everyday objects.

- Will we source props or make our own?

- Will the figures be in a natural setting or in one that we have created with our images (drawn/photographed or sourced from books or the Internet)?

- Will we be leaving the 'scenes' out in the open, in the manner of Slinkachu, or packing them away, in the manner of Cordal?

- The figures do not always stand up on their own – how will we overcome this?

- The figures are very delicate – how will we avoid damaging them?

In order to develop this into a joint photography and literacy project, introduce the idea of the 'little people' as actual characters and allow pupils to choose their own 'person'. This should be done in groups or pairs (always together – this is a collaborative activity where pupils need to discuss and develop their ideas). You can give the pupils some prompts or ideas that they might want to think about or you can simply leave this completely open ended. Here are some characteristics pupils could consider:

- Name

- Age

- Where they live

- Job

- Friends

- Favourite saying

- Secret

- Likes/dislikes

- Possessions

- Problems

Basically, you are just trying to get pupils to be creative and unleash their imaginations. With some groups you may want to model this and create a 'story' for one of your own characters.

Here is an example for Gladys, who is the homeless figure in the image opposite pushing a trolley.

Gladys

Home

Gladys is homeless and wanders around the streets. She carries all of her belongings in a supermarket trolley which is beginning to rust.

Possessions

Her most treasured possession is a tatty old photograph album. It has black and white photos of two young boys

House

She sleeps where she can – sometimes under the bridge near the canal but with the recent floods it's now too soggy, so she has to sleep in the park – she doesn't like this as much because she doesn't feel safe there.

Friends

She doesn't have any real friends, although she does speak to Bert sometimes when she passes his bench.

Her secret

She had a really important job but made a mistake and lost lots of money – her family do not know where she is although they have searched and placed adverts in newspapers trying to find her.

Likes and dislikes

She doesn't like the people who make fun of her – especially that group of teenagers who shout at her whenever she passes them.

She loves chocolate but can't remember when she last had some.

Problem

A problem that she has to face is dealing with the cold, her coat is now very thin and her boots have holes in them.

Favourite saying

'I wish I could turn the clock back'

147

My character

Home

Possessions

House

Friends

Name

Likes and dislikes

Their secret

Problem

Favourite saying

The image of Gladys on page 147 is another image taken by pupils.

In this case, I have deliberately left gaps and hooks to allow pupils to ask questions. For inspiration, consider what sort of questions could be generated from Gladys's example:

- Who are the two young boys in the photograph?

- Why do you not feel safe sleeping in the park?

- How long have you been living on the streets?

- What frightens you the most?

- What job did you used to do?

- Did you make a mistake at work?

- Do you miss your family?

- Do you think your family miss you?

- Why don't you contact your family?

- Are you wanted by the police?

- Where do you get your food?

- Where do you have a wash?

- What is in your trolley?

- Do you know why your trolley is rusting?

This list is just a quick one – your pupils will have a lot more questions. Perhaps you could ask the class if they are happy for you to go into role as 'Gladys' and answer their questions. This then allows a dialogue to develop and Gladys's story really comes to life.

Once the pupils understand her background and have some idea of her story, they can then write and create the scenes for a storybook. Storybooks or storyboards can be created by taking individual images and then mounting them onto a large sheet of card. Alternatively, pupils could use apps such as Comic Life or Creative Book Builder to create their stories.

Once pupils have created Gladys's story, you can expand in several ways.

Create the background to Gladys's life

- Draw a map of where Gladys goes in the town – label key areas, photograph this and add to your storybook.

- Identify her sleeping area then photograph the figure *in situ*.

- Use modelling clay/Fimo/Plasticine and any other scraps to a create scene for her to be photographed in.

- Create a tableau in which Gladys meets the teenagers – freeze-frame and photograph (you can use the app ToonPAINT to turn these into cartoons – see Chapter 4).

- Create a scene where Gladys meets the teenagers, including dialogue (this will encourage empathy).

- Write a diary extract of Gladys's day.

- Film a monologue of a pupil in role as Gladys explaining her day.

- Write a letter to Gladys from her family.

- Create a newspaper front page from the day when she made her 'big mistake' – include photographs.

- Write or film a dialogue between Gladys and Bert.

- Where will Gladys be this time next year? What problems might she have to face? Write her story or create it using an app such as Creative Book Builder or Comic Life.

- Research life on the streets, the *Big Issue* and what help is available for homeless people. Turn this into a poster using an app such as Phoster

- Read *A Street Cat named Bob* by James Bowen,[6] or watch extracts on YouTube.

This list is just to give you some ideas, but it is also important to let pupils generate their own ideas and go with them wherever possible.

> Taylor's Toy Company has commissioned you to create point-of-sale posters for 'little people'. They would like a whole range of packaging ideas and they would like the figures to feature in the packaging.

Taking little people outdoors

I've used the little person that my pupils call 'Bert' for this section, but many of the little people would be equally, if not more, appropriate. Bert is a solitary character sitting on a bench with three coloured bags at his side. I always assume that he is homeless, but it may be that pupils decide he is merely resting on his way home from the shops and his bags are heavy. (I realise that I think of these characters as people but try to remember that they are, in fact, only props!)

Outdoor learning is recognised as having a positive impact, especially on younger children. However, being in the fresh air and working in a different way may well be the stimulus that some pupils need to spark their interest. Different materials are readily available if you move your learning to an outside space.

In the examples provided, I haven't actually created a 'space' – I've merely placed Bert in different locations. Taking my inspiration from Slinkachu, I have photographed him twice in each location, once close up and once to take in more of the surrounding area.

---

6 J. Bowen, *A Street Cat Named Bob: How One Man and His Cat Found Hope on the Streets* (London: Hodder & Stoughton, 2012).

Images inspired by Slinkachu's work in *Little People in the City*.

Challenge the pupils to create an outdoor environment in which to photograph their little person. The different characters that you might find useful are:

- Climbers

- Painters

- Crime investigators

- The graffiti artist

- Hikers

- Photographers

- 'Trying to find' (see the bubble image on page 199)

- Woman with lawn mower

- Boats and people

- People gardening with tools

- Angler in boat

- People in deckchairs

Pupils will need to photograph their scenes (such as the one opposite) in order to create story-boards and storybooks for them. Different figures will clearly require different settings – will the angler be in a puddle, on a piece of shiny litter, on a glass surface or washed up on sand? What are the crime scene investigators looking at: a flower with all of its petals removed (make sure it's a daisy not a prize bloom!) or an insect which is obviously much bigger than them (probably not a wasp!)? It would be interesting to do this in different seasons and see what the same image looks like in the snow, or with autumn leaves or with snails.

Remember to address any pertinent safety issues, not least if you are using these figures with young children, but common sense is key rather than hundreds of health and safety regulations. If you feel these little figures are too small, then Lego figures would work just as well. You could also use a favourite figure, teddy bear or toy in exactly the same manner. You could even link this to books you are reading in class – for example, the pupils could create their own 'Flat Stanley'.

See Chapter 4: iPhoneography and apps

Time-lapse apps

Use iPads and time-lapse apps (such as iLapse) to film your work in setting up scenes and taking images outdoors.

One photo out of focus is a mistake, ten photos out of focus are an experiment, one hundred photos out of focus – that's a style.

Anonymous

Chapter 10

Photo challenges

Photography lends itself to the setting of challenges. The challenges in this chapter are varied, both in approach and audience, but they all have several aims in common:

- They involve high challenge but low stress.

- They are creative and push thinking, but you can't get them wrong – interpretation of the challenges is actively encouraged.

- Creative and off-the-wall thinking to create inspiring images.

- Discussion prior to pupils taking the photographs and then about the images they have taken will help to develop their ideas and confidence.

The challenges can take place for just a few minutes each day or could easily be made into a whole day or week's challenge, depending upon how you want to approach them.

> Put pupils into groups and give them one hour to take twenty-six photos, each beginning with a different letter of the alphabet.

#Photochallenge30

The list of topics to the right outlines the #Photochallenge30 for pupils.

#Photochallenge30 developed from working with a group of teachers via Twitter who were all undertaking a 365 photography project – that is, taking an image a day for a whole year. In order to make this seem less daunting for all involved, it was broken down into monthly lists of ideas for each day. In turn, this led to the creation of a thirty-day challenge for pupils.

#Photochallenge30 includes thirty prompts and suggestions for specific photographs to be taken on a daily basis. The challenge can be approached in a variety of ways. Many of the topic areas can be taken simply at face value, but they can also be used to provoke discussion and consider more metaphorical ideas. For example, the topic of day 11 is 'a secret'.

How can the pupils take a photograph of a secret? Is it symbolic (e.g. an image of a lock and keys)? Is it someone whispering in the ear of another person? Is it a diary? The classroom discussion can be far-reaching. Is a secret still a secret if you only tell one person? It is important to stress to pupils that any interpretation of the prompt is allowed as long as they can explain their thinking. Number 18 is

#photochallenge30 for pupils

1. Through the window 2. Hands
3. Anything beginning with the letter H
4. Words 5. LOCAL AREA 6. A NUMBER
7. CLASSROOM 8. FRIENDS 9. Doors
10. Something that made you smile
11. A SECRET 12. Your teacher
13. A book that you love 14. A FACELESS PORTRAIT
15. Someone you admire 16. ARTWORK
17. Beauty 18. Learning
19. Out of focus
20. The sky's the limit
21. Teamwork 22. something blue 23. Texture
24. Shadows 25. Laughter
26. Reflections
27. DREAMS AND HOPES 28. A Message
29. Memories
30. ALL OF YOUR CLASS

'learning' – it will be interesting to see what image pupils produce to show what learning looks like in your classroom.

One Year 2 class did this challenge as a half-term project. (Parents were fully involved and their class blog had over 150 comments during the week.) When faced with day 7, 'classroom', they had to be really creative as they were not actually at school. Many took photographs of their toys placed in a classroom setting that they had created, but one pupil uploaded a collage of themselves in different locations with the caption: 'Everywhere is a classroom because I learn everywhere'. Amazing!

You could upload your #photochallenge to your class blog or a free photo-hosting site, such as the ones below (these are just some examples). Then you can work with other schools and see how other pupils have interpreted the challenges.

- www.shuttercal.com – this free site allows you to upload an image a day onto a calendar. You can see other people's calendars and follow them in the same way that you would on other social media sites. If you wish, you can pay to have the images printed to fit into a shoebox. Alternatively, you can print them off yourself and use them in scrapbooks.

- http://365project.org – this is another free site that contains discussion boards and weekly competitions. Obviously these are optional – you can start at your own pace and simply use the site to host your images.

- http://www.blipfoto.com – this a photo journal community where you upload an image a day. An accompanying blog also contains top tips and advice.

Using online sites and blogs gives other teachers and children a chance to comment on images, which then gives pupils a genuine audience for their work. It also means that parents can be involved too. When trialling this technique, I received questions and comments from pupils and teachers alike. There is something very special about having a conversation with a Year 2 pupil via Twitter about how she could put a border onto her photograph and then receiving a very polite thank you.

Many pupils will ask for or feel more confident with some rules. We all need some structures in our work, but this is an ideal opportunity for pupils and teacher to work together. What rules do *we* (note the pronoun) want? This is *our* challenge – it's exciting and *we* will agree on *our* approach (it's not something that the teacher sets as a task). The givens can be discussed and negotiated, but I would recommend keeping them simple and achievable – if we focus too heavily on the practicalities, we are in danger of losing the spontaneity of the challenge.

   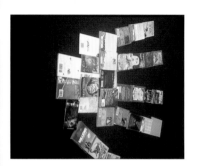

The examples above from primary pupils all show imagination: they evidence decision-making and collaboration as well as technical skills in actually taking the photograph (and manipulating it in some cases).

For day 2, 'hands', a Key Stage 2 group commented on the image below: 'To create "Many hands make a loving family", we used an iPhone and added the Toaster filter from Instagram.'

It would be interesting to do a school yearbook project with your class using the #Photochallenge30 format. You could purchase a cheap digital camera at the start of the year and then pass this round, in turn, so each pupil (and yourself) takes an image every thirty or so days. It would be a great way to share what you are doing and what is happening in school.

It would also be good to allow the children to take the camera home. Pupils could create their own guidelines and this will encourage shared responsibility. They will need to be accountable for the care of the actual camera but also for the image content – for example, what do they consider to be 'appropriate' subject matter? If they are going to take images of people, should they ask for permission?

You could get pupils to write an explanation, short sentence or poem, or find a quote to add to their image. Many sites on the Internet will actually publish a book in hard copy as well as create a virtual online copy to share with parents and the community. Schools who undertook the #Photochallenge30 with pupils found that this had spin-offs into other areas, such as links with parents, e-safety discussions and literacy projects. The teacher of one class admitted that she was stumped for an idea on day 3 – something beginning with the letter H. The idea of hopscotch and the photo below came without prompting.

Skills covered by pupils undertaking #Photochallenge30

- Following a brief and interpreting it
- Teamwork – negotiating rules and structures/taking images
- Evaluating apps
- Use of ICT – image editing software/blogging
- Creativity
- Communication with adults – teachers/parents
- Explaining their choice of image
- Analysis of images from others in their class and/or other classes undertaking this challenge

The out-of-focus shot was a 'happy accident', but it sparked a valuable discussion about e-safety and the posting of images in appropriate online forums. (This proves a useful reminder that, as teachers, we don't have to have all of the answers and it's good to let pupils take the lead sometimes.)

In pairs, take three photographs of your partner: one looking happy, one confused and one sad. Use these to create cards to put next to you whilst you are working so that the teacher knows if you understand what you are doing.

Using apps to edit #Photochallenge30

It quickly became apparent that pupils wanted to edit the work they had produced as part of the challenge and were very comfortable in sourcing and using photographic apps (see also Chapter 4).

> See Chapter 4: iPhoneography and apps
>
> **Using apps**

As they become more familiar with apps, pupils will begin to evaluate them and want more sophistication and add-ons (e.g. borders, effects, stamps, labels, text, grunge, collage effects, filters). New apps can be introduced and pupils can then be encouraged to work out how to use them without instruction from you.

This process could be formalised and pupils could create their own 'good apps guide' for photography, using an app such as Creative Book Builder. Pairs of pupils could become experts in a particular app and become the specialists other pupils go to for help, rather than the teacher being the one with all knowledge. They could then design their own slogans and badges to wear (with photographs on them, obviously!) or labels for their desk:

Snap to it – I'm your Snapseed expert.

It's not old, it's Vintage – ask me about Vintique.

I'm sure their ideas will be a lot more creative!

Pupils could have an 'app of the week' and take it in turns to produce a display or talk. They could then analyse professional reviews or review apps themselves. Encourage them to look at the use of language in reviews: why are the descriptions on the apps themselves always 'glowing'? Are there any contrasts between what the app description says and what the reviewers say? Why do they think that is?

If they are going to give their apps a star rating, the class will have to decide what each star means and produce their own criteria. What do they think are important features (e.g. good design, usability, add-ons)?

> Give all pupils the same image and ask them to edit it using an app or apps of their choice.

> Write a review of an app – then go online and compare your review to those written by other users.

#photochallenge12 for teachers

1. A lightbulb moment

2. favourite quote

3. THE REASON I TEACH

4. Something that made you smile today ...

5. A teacher is ...

6. KEEP CALM AND ...

7. All teachers should read this

8. A meeting

9. The WRITTEN WORD

10. I want my pupils to be ...

11. All teachers should have ...

12. How I want my pupils to remember me ...

Be creative, have fun - think outside the box.

Remember - there are no wrong answers!

#Photochallenge12

As many teachers enjoyed doing #Photochallenge30 with their pupils, this was developed and a separate challenge was created just for teachers – #Photochallenge12.

If you decide to attempt this challenge, remember that you are doing this for two reasons. One is to put yourself in the position of a learner and participant in order to develop empathy with your pupils. The other is to challenge yourself – how imaginative can you be? How do you sum up the day 5 challenge, 'A teacher is ...', in a single photograph?

> Take the #Photochallenge12 for teachers – challenge yourself!

Calendar challenge

This is called the 'calendar challenge' but it could easily be adapted to any other sort of publication. This is a collaborative activity that works well on a development day or when you are giving your pupils a task to be completed by a clear deadline.

The object of this exercise is for pupils to work in groups – completely independently of their teacher – to design, create and produce a calendar that can be sold for charity. The brief is as open-ended as that, but it covers a whole range of skills and subjects.

The key thing to remember is to give the pupils autonomy. If they make mistakes, that's OK – it's up to them to spot the mistakes, rectify them and learn from them. On one occasion, I could clearly see that one group were not working as a team and, as a result, two sub-teams were both working on the December page. My instinct was to jump in and point this out – I almost had to sit on my hands to stop myself from interfering. You could argue that I was wrong and I could have saved them time by pointing it out. Had I done so, I feel that this would have resulted in an argument and them blaming one another so as not to lose face in front of me. As it was, one of them spotted their mistake and they worked together to sort it out – this showed them, and me, that they could do it without my help.

Once groups have been established, they need to consider the following areas: theme, charity, roles/skills, costing and funding, and marketing,

Theme

Their calendar will first need a theme:

- Will it be seasonal (i.e. each month focuses on what is happening, so February is Valentine's Day)?

- Will it be 'local' (with photographs of attractive scenes from the local area)?

- Will it have specific subject matter (maybe linked to their chosen charity, e.g. children) or a colour scheme?

The groups then need to decide how they select their theme (will they each have a vote?) and, most importantly, assess whether the idea is marketable. This final part underpins the whole exercise and it is important to give pupils time to discuss and negotiate. You can chip in with pertinent questions where necessary (e.g. if you are going to be taking the photographs yourself, is choosing polar bears as your theme the best idea?).

Will we sell more calendars by using amazing professional images that do not necessarily 'mean' anything to our school and parents, or by using images that we have taken ourselves that maybe aren't as professional but have the 'personal touch'?

See Chapter 1: Camera basics

Copyright and the use of Creative Commons images

It might be a good idea to introduce the concept of copy-right before beginning this work (see Chapter 1). A discussion on this will be necessary if the pupils want to use images taken by others. If you search for Creative Commons images on the Internet, this will lead you to images that are free to use in both educational and commercial settings.

Charity

Next, the pupils need to decide which charity they will support. They should consider whether they want to support a local or a national charity. How will they decide? Do any of them have a personal link to a charity? Are they willing to share this with their teammates? This can be a very powerful discussion but relies upon trust and empathy within the group.

They will need to work as a team to evaluate their ideas and negotiate to come to a decision. Do they need to research this further? Is this a specific role for someone within the group? Will the charity that they choose have an impact upon the style and content of their calendar?

Roles/skills

Are pupils going to have specific roles? If you have worked with techniques such as Spencer Kagan's cooperative learning strategies[1] or Dorothy Heathcote's Mantle of the Expert,[2] then pupils will find the idea of roles well within their comfort zone.

They will need to discuss what roles might be required in a calendar production company. Ask them to make their own lists – it may be that they have to take on more than one role each depending on group sizes. Examples *could* include the following (but don't give this list to pupils as they may just adopt it without thinking it through for themselves):

- Photographer
- Layout designer/editor
- Marketing expert
- Accountant
- Quality controller
- Researcher
- Director with overall control
- Charity expert
- Secretary

How will they decide who does what role? Throughout this task pupils need to learn to work together and play to their strengths. They will gain confidence as the challenge progresses and they can see the finished result emerging.

---

1 See <http://www.kaganonline.com/index.php>.
2 See <http://www.mantleoftheexpert.com/>.

Costing and funding

In real life, money is a key factor, so to keep this challenge as realistic as possible, financing is an issue that the pupils will need to address. It is important that they make the link between how much the calendar will cost to produce, the quality of the finished product, the sale price and the profit to be made for their charity.

This is a high-level skill. Do they produce it cheaply and sell it at a low price point? What is their target market? Is it better to have a high-quality product which sells fewer copies but is more expensive? This will rely on their accountant producing spreadsheets and costings for them to discuss. The quality controller will need to focus on this too – if the calendar is not up to standard then it obviously won't sell.

Will they have the calendar produced in-house? If so, they will need to speak to your reprographics department. If they are going to have it printed commercially, what are the cost implications? Do they need a sponsor to fund their original outlay? If so, who will it be? Who could they approach? This may require a professional letter or phone call made by the pupils themselves.

Note that it is the pupils themselves who have to make the decisions and approach sponsors or the reprographics department – this project is *their* responsibility. They will act like professionals if you treat them in this way. It is interesting that it is often the adult with whom they are dealing that will struggle when discussing planning and strategies with pupils rather than the other way round!

Marketing

Marketing will follow on naturally from costings and funding. It will need to be included as a cost, but that may not occur to pupils until later – in which case, they will have to readjust their costs.

Where will they market the calendar? Whether it is the school website, the local paper, local radio, flyers or their own blog, this will require literacy and ICT skills.

They may wish to have a launch event, which will require planning and resourcing in the same manner as the original calendar challenge.

> What other photographic items could you create and sell?
>
> Research online photographic companies such as Photobox and Snapfish for some ideas.

Album cover challenge

If this is to be a real task with a real outcome, then pupils have to be aware of their deadlines. They must be responsible for quality control – if their project is not saleable they will be responsible – so they need organisational skills as well as creative ones. This is a brilliant way to encourage enterprise skills alongside their photography – I only hope that you don't get too many requests to recreate (or star in) a Women's Institute *Calendar Girl*-style calendar!

> Create a school newsletter or a flyer for the **PE** department to advertise extra-curricular activities.
>
> You could look at online sites, such as www.smore.com, for some ideas.

Many good ideas can be found on the forums of the 365 photography sites mentioned above (see page 157) – the inspiration for the album challenge comes from 365project.org. The idea is to create a specific album cover for a fictitious band, with clear instructions about how to come up with the band name.

First, go to Wikipedia and hit 'random article' – you now have the name of your band. To get the name of your album, visit any quotations website (such as http://thedailyquotes.com or www.brainyquote.com) and use the last four or five words of any quote. This creates some really random titles – try it! These instructions generated the band name Billy the Cat and Kate, with the album title 'A Friend is a Gift You Give Yourself'. This selection is workable, but some are so totally off the wall that it is as well to give pupils the choice of hitting the refresh button three times and choosing the best option.

Then ask them to create an album cover for their band.

Note: with thanks to Sarah in my adult education class for this example.

Book cover challenge

As an alternative to an album cover, you could ask pupils to design a book jacket. An easier way to do this might be to use a random title generator – there are several of these available if you Google this term. Using a couple of random generators, I was given the following titles:

The Seventh Butterfly

White Window

Silent School

Forgotten Secrets

However, as you have no control over any random generator – they are totally random! – it might be a good idea to do this beforehand and print off a list of titles for pupils to pick out of a box. They can then set about designing their covers.

Another way to get pupils to create book covers would be to give them a list of classic book titles to pick from, but don't tell them what the book is about. *Persuasion, Hard Times, The Thirty-Nine Steps, Pride and Prejudice, Great Expectations, Lord of the Flies, Watership Down, 1984, The Road to Wigan Pier, Animal Farm, Holes* – the list is endless! Obviously, you can use whatever titles you wish but it would be interesting to see what pupils produce for these literary classics.

Only when they have taken their photographs and created their book covers should you get them to search for a synopsis of the book – or better still read it! How appropriate is their cover? Perhaps find some genuine book jackets and compare them with the pupils' – this would make an amazing display and would generate discussion. This could be done with both adult and children's books.

This could serve as an interesting link to your literacy work – can the pupils recreate the front cover for the one of the books that you are reading as a class? You could also create a front cover for a set of stories written by the class.

Create a photo card which could be sent home as a 'praise card'. Think about image, size, text and layout.

The whole point of taking pictures is so that you don't have to explain things with words.

Elliott Erwitt

Chapter 11

All about me

Self-portraits

A self-portrait can be a way of showing others how you view yourself. It can be notoriously difficult to describe your character – people are often loathe to do so for fear of seeming smug or self-important.

As adults, we rarely see ourselves as others do and are often much more critical of ourselves than others are. I have an amazing friend who is creative and talented – she writes brilliant poems and diary extracts which are funny and clever takes on life. She has no idea of her own talent or of how much we all love her work and rely on her candid and often refreshing point of view. Conversely, I have another friend who was horrified when at a staff INSET, during which we were asked to describe our colleagues as if they were animals (always a risk!), she was described as a shark. No amount of pleading, 'But I'm a dolphin', changed people's minds. Our perception of ourselves is often nothing like the view that others have of us.

However, producing a visual self-portrait can give us more scope to express ourselves. I'm not talking here about the photographs that populate Facebook and the like – of people taking 'selfies' or photographs of themselves in mirrors with their phones just before they go out (or, even worse, after they've been out for a while!). Instead, the image should focus on an aspect of your personality – such as your character, likes, a defining trait or prized possession – or it could be a favourite quote which sums up your outlook on life. There are no rules – it should just be something which shows an aspect of you in visual form.

There was an interesting article in the *Cape Times* in 2012 about selfies (i.e. the self-portrait captured with an outstretched arm, usually using a smartphone), which has been described as one of the most iconic photo poses of the internet age. The newspaper manipulated some famous historical images, such as the Duke and Duchess of Cambridge kissing on the balcony after the royal wedding, to make it look as if they have been taken as selfies![1]

You could approach the self-portrait in several ways:

1   Simply give pupils cameras and no instructions other than 'take a self-portrait'. Then analyse the results. Why did they take the images they did in the way that they did? Ask them to choose the image that they think sums them up most effectively, print these out and create a whole-class collage that you can again analyse. Does the class think the self-portraits are accurate? Are they only showing the 'face' that the individuals want us to see? Do they see themselves differently to the way their peers see them?
Note: even though this is a self-portrait, there is nothing to stop pupils setting up the image and then actually asking another pupil to actually press the shutter (unless you have the funds to buy remote releases for your cameras).

2   Ask pupils to work in threes – they should write six words to describe themselves then another six words to describe each of the other two. They should then use these words to compare and discuss how they see themselves and how others see them.

Next, they should choose the one word that, as a three, they agree sums up each person. The pupils should then use this word to help with the planning of their own self-portrait – the word would influence the setting, the background and any props.

Take a photograph that sums up a particular person without including the person themselves. You could add one or more constraints to make pupils think more deeply:

●   It must not include the person's face.

●   It must be black and white.

●   It must include at least one prop.

●   It must be taken with the person wearing a mask so we learn about them from their body language/props/ location. (White plastic theatre-style masks can be bought very cheaply online and work well when looking at poses and body language.)

●   It must be a photograph of a reflection – e.g. reflected in a camera lens, mirror, tin foil, water or even a door handle.

●   It must be overlaid with a textures layer – the combined image must sum up the person.

1   See <http://adsoftheworld.com/media/print/the_cape_times_william>.

Ideas

Once the whole class has taken a self-portrait you could then use these images as a stimulus for written work and display. Give each pupil an A4 sheet to include both the image and their writing (in whatever form – it need only be a couple of words, a poem or a quote). You can then have these spiral bound as a class book.

If you are going to create a display with the self-portraits, then think big and use a whole wall. Make a real statement and have the images printed as A3 or bigger. Alternatively, give each pupil a luggage tag – they should paste their image on one side and add their writing on the other side. The tags can then be suspended from a branch or rope in the classroom. Or the class could create a tree and hang the tags onto the branches. Another idea is to decorate wooden pegs and use these to hang the images on a piece of string around the top of the walls or across the ceiling of the classroom.

Pupils could turn their photos (with or without writing) into a class movie (Windows Movie Maker and Photo Story 3 are both free) or, if you have Macs or iPads, iMovie is excellent. They could write the voice-over script or choose the music that sums them up as a class.

If you are doing the self-portrait activity with younger pupils, you could put the photos into a memory box (obviously get the pupils to design this) to be opened when they leave school. You can then expand this into considering where would be a safe place to keep the box to avoid damage to the photographs.

The photograph overleaf is of twins. They were happy about having their photographs taken but also wanted to see them printed off. They were amazed at their photos but then just giggled and 'swapped faces' for this photograph.

Is it our outward appearance that is most important or something indefinable that makes us unique? Years ago there was a play which was all staged around a hospital bed. The man in the bed had been in an accident and had basically been given a brain transplant. There was a woman at either side of the bed – one was the wife of the 'body' the other was the wife of the 'brain'. Whose husband was he?

What actually makes us what we are? What makes us unique?

It's one thing to make a picture of what a person looks like.
It's another thing to make a portrait of who they are.

Paul Caponigro

The golden ratio and beauty

The golden ratio, also known by the Greek letter *phi*, has been the basis of much mathematical and scientific research. Its value is approximately equal to 1.618 and it has been used throughout human history – such as by the Egyptian mathematicians who designed Great Pyramid of Giza and the Greek sculptor Phidias in his statues at the Parthenon. In basic terms, the long side of a rectangle would have to be 1.6 times bigger than the short side for it to fit the golden ratio.

The golden ratio has been used to analyse the proportions of natural objects, such as animals and plants. It has also been used by architects, musicians, artists and designers to bring a pleasing sense of proportion to their work. It is thought that the closer something is to the golden ratio, the more pleasurable it is to the human eye. In the 1860s, a German scientist called Gustav Fechner carried out some basic experiments using different sized rectangles. In his study, over three-quarters of the people involved chose the rectangles which were closest to the golden ratio in their proportions as the most visually pleasing.

The principle is believed to be the same with regard to the human face. People are drawn to faces which fit most closely to the golden ratio and these are perceived as the most 'beautiful'. If you measure the width of the eyes and the length of the face on the *Mona Lisa*, for example, the face is 1.6 times longer than the width. Our brains are 'wired' to find this ratio aesthetically pleasing.

By measuring the width and length of faces, as well as a whole host of other key measurements, we can determine how closely they conform to this ratio. This would make for a great joint maths and photography project.

Ideas

- Take headshot images from magazines or the Internet and measure these from hairline to chin and across the eyes to work out how close they are to the golden ratio.

- Once you have worked out how close they are to the ratio, conduct a survey to see which faces people regard as beautiful. Do your findings support the above theory?

- Can you find examples of people who are deemed to be 'beautiful' but who do not have faces which conform to the golden ratio (apparently this includes Angelina Jolie!).

- Show the pupils an image of the *Mona Lisa* and ask them to find out whether this fits with the golden ratio.

- Studies have shown that a haircut can alter the ratio of a person's face, so someone can look better or worse after a haircut – discuss! You could try to find images of 'beautiful celebrities' with a variety of hairstyles and see if you can prove or disprove this theory.

- Produce a photographic collage to show 'beauty' – what will you include?

- Produce one image which you feel sums up the concept of 'beauty' (this could be symbolic).

Other discussion questions could include: what is beauty? Can beauty be defined by a mathematical formula? Should we judge by outward appearance or is 'beauty' what is on the inside?

Beauty can be seen in all things ... seeing and composing the beauty is what separates the snapshot from the photograph.

Matt Hardy

Which is your best side?

Kelsey Blackburn and James Schirillo from Wake Forest University, in North Carolina, have produced a study which shows that images of the left-hand side of a person's face are more pleasing than those of the right-hand side.[2] They argue that this is because more emotion is shown on the left side of the face. This would be an interesting premise upon which to base a class experiment.

> Research shows that the left hand side of a person's face makes for a more pleasing photograph.
>
> How could you test this hypothesis?
>
> Do your findings agree with this hypothesis?

Photography often allows people to express themselves in a way that they would perhaps be too self-conscious to do in another format. For example, asking students to hold up chalkboards which portray their hopes for the year ahead can be a great ice-breaker at the beginning of a school year. Photographs are then taken of all the pupils holding their boards. These could be in terms of what job they are aiming for, what their life goal is and so on – it always forms the basis for a good discussion. Whilst some of the outcomes are as expected, there are always students who think deeply and come up with very philosophical answers. When carrying this out with a group of over 400 Year 9 students, answers ranged from break-dancer to God and from hairdresser to ninja! In the midst of all the comments about whether they would rather be rich or happy – a discussion in itself – one girl simply wrote 'Me' on her chalkboard. How profound for a 13-year-old.

The chalkboard photographs can then be used to create a huge wall display where parents are encouraged to 'find their child' when visiting. This also allows for discussion at the end of the year, or even at the end of their school journey – what has changed?

Staff can join in too, which gives you a chance to show your human side and that you have a sense of humour. You could also adapt the chalkboard idea for your 'Meet Our Staff Board' as in the image opposite.

The only props that you need are a plain wall and a set of chalkboards or whiteboards. The 'speech bubble' ones are more expensive, but the square ones will cost around 99p (including chalk) from a pound shop. Alternatively, pupils could make their shaped speech bubble boards from MDF and blackboard paint, with help from the DT or art department.

---

2   K. Blackburn and J. Schirillo, Emotive Hemispheric Differences Measured in Real-Life Portraits Using Pupil Diameter and Subjective Aesthetic Preferences, *Experimental Brain Research* 219(4) (2012): 447–455.

A photograph is a secret about a secret.
The more it tells you the less you know.

Diane Arbus

Messages

Take the idea of using the chalkboards further and ask pupils to think about a message that they would like to share. It has to be their message and they have to be able to capture this in a photograph. You could give them a steer to begin with some examples like the one below.

Listen to the hand

Pupils work in groups to decide what they feel strongly about or what worries them. This has to be summed up in a message which is short enough to fit onto their hand. This has the advantage of allowing less confident students to literally 'hide behind their hand'. It would also work if the message is a little controversial and is making the student feel a little nervous. They only get one message so it has to be something that they feel strongly about. It may be that you organise a session discussing lots of ideas in advance, but then pupils have to prioritise and make a clear choice.

The teacher could introduce the statements below to start off a discussion:

1 I worry about my health.

2 I worry about letting people down.

3 I worry that my appearance is not what I want it to be.

4 I worry about the future.

5 I worry that my friends will all achieve more than I will.

6 I worry too much about what other people think of me.

7 I worry about the state of the planet in the future.

8 I worry that there won't be a job for me.

9 I worry that I won't meet my soulmate.

These statements could then be used in a diamond nine exercise, where pupils arrange the statements into a diamond shape – with the statement they deem to be the most worrying on the top row, the next level of seriousness on row two, the three they worry less about on the middle row and followed by the two and one that they worry about least.

> This hand activity will lead into a discussion about how much of ourselves we are willing to reveal to other people. Some questions to start off the discussion might be:
>
> - Does everyone have secrets?
>
> - Are some secrets harder to keep than others?
>
> - Has anyone ever said to you: 'This is meant to be a secret so don't tell anyone'? How does that make you feel? What did you do?
>
> - Why do people keep some things secret?

Another reason that this activity works well is simply because you are allowing/encouraging students to write on their hands! However, you could also think about other ways of photographing a message. Here are some examples:

- A steamed up mirror or window.

- A Scrabble board or Scrabble letters

- A white mug and permanent marker

- A sticky note

- A torn scrap of paper

- A text message on the screen of a mobile phone

- Luggage labels

- Torn letters from a newspaper – ransom-note style

- T-shirt slogan

- Chalk message on the floor

- A newspaper with everything blacked out except key words

Chapter 12

Independent learning

Why independent learning?

Photography lends itself to individual expression and sometimes pupils need to be able to work independently and develop their own ideas. Some of the projects covered in this book rely on pupils expressing their personal ideas and giving insights into their 'world'. By creating an extended independent learning task, you are freeing pupils from some of the limits that they often face in school. For example, timing and resources are an issue in all subject areas. Photography can add additional constraints, such as the right light conditions and accessibility to the people and places that pupils want to include in their photographs. However, these can be overcome more readily if the pupils are working independently and managing their own time.

By allocating longer periods of time for independent work, you are allowing for periods of reflection and development. There are times in lessons when the focus can become the task itself and not the creative process or the resourcefulness of pupils. The task in this chapter is just one example of how photography can be used to allow pupils to develop their time management, organisational, creative and reflective skills.

It is a good idea to communicate the task to parents and ask that they support and work with their children. However, be aware that when asking parents whether they have helped their children to complete extended tasks that they can become defensive – as if they *shouldn't* help. In fact, being able to discuss their work with a supportive adult is a mature skill that we should be encouraging in our pupils.

The task we are focusing on in this chapter is a photo essay. You may wish to call it something else – decide for yourself after reading the brief. As with all good learning, hooking pupils in and gaining their interest is important. Having worked with advanced skills teacher Debra Kidd on several occasions, she always stresses that pupils should be 'protected into' their work. If we just throw them a load of instructions, however carefully worded, they will either sink or swim; they will 'get it' or be 'switched off'. By planning our way in with care, we can hopefully avoid some of the pitfalls that pupils might face.

The way in

The children's brief for this project will be as follows: to produce a photo essay about their life. They will need to include at least six images (but no more than ten). They should think carefully about these as each one needs to count. Each image must say something about their life. They may choose to add text or the images can stand alone. The presentation of their work is completely their choice. The audience for the photo essay will be the curator of an exhibition entitled 'It's My Life', which is a collection of work that aims to show the life of young people in the early twenty-first century.

It is best not to share the brief with the pupils at this stage. Instead, the way in is focused on the life of young people in Uganda. Having been fortunate to visit and work in schools there, this is based on first-hand experience.

> What do we mean by 'culture'?
>
> How can this be expressed in photographs?

Give pupils the image opposite and ask them to SIFT it (see Chapter 9). The 'seeing' part of the SIFT process is very important here, as they will use this to assess what a classroom is like in Uganda.

> See Chapter 7: Visual literacy
> **SIFT**

What can pupils *see* in this image? The list below could be used as prompts by the teacher but may well not be necessary:

- The desks are narrow and uneven.

- The floor is made of mud.

- A drain runs down the side of the classroom.

- The classroom is dark and has very little natural light – the window has no glass in it.

- There is no evidence of any technology or any electricity.

In the discussion that follows, the pupils could *infer* what they think it would be like to be at school in Uganda as opposed to their own school.

Next, set small groups of pupils the task of preparing a lesson for the Ugandan schoolchildren on a subject of your choice – anything from a geography lesson about the continents to a poetry lesson. Once the pupils have created their lesson plan, ask them to teach this to another group within the class.

In their groups, ask pupils to look again at the image of the Ugandan classroom and identify any problems that they might encounter with their resources and with the lesson itself if they were teaching in that setting.

The following comments *may* help the teacher:

- The tables are very narrow and uneven which will make writing difficult.

- If you look at the photograph carefully there are no pens and only a couple of sheets of paper.

- The walls are damp, so nothing will stick to them.

- Resources are scarce and in many cases there are *no* resources (e.g. paper, pens, crayons, chalk).

- There is no electricity which means very little light, no computers or whiteboards.

Allow pupils time to reflect and adapt their lesson in the light of the issues and difficulties they have discussed.

> Show the children the image opposite and ask them to think about the differences between their home and the one in Uganda.

Schools in Uganda

Next, use the SIFT model again to get the pupils to analyse the images opposite and answer the following questions:

- Does this montage work as a series of stand-alone images?

- Do the images raise questions?

- Are they thought provoking?

- Is it an honest portrayal of life in Uganda? Does it give a balanced view?

- Is there an image you think is missing (e.g. an aspect of school life in Uganda that you want to see)?

- If you added text – what would you say?

The brief

You can now introduce the photo essay brief to the pupils.

> Produce a 'photo essay' about your life. You will need to include at least six images but no more than ten – think carefully about these as each one needs to count. Each image must tell me something about your life. You may choose to add text or you may feel that the images are strong enough to stand alone. The presentation of your work is completely your choice.

It is important that timescale, practicalities and levels of parental involvement are then negotiated with pupils.

Timescale

- How long will you work on this project?

- Do you want to build in reflection points?

- Can you agree upon a deadline?

Practicalities

- Do you need to borrow equipment? If so, from whom?

- Can you agree upon systems for borrowing equipment?

- Can you use phones/your own cameras?

Involvement

- How will you involve your parents?

- Is the work going to be 'assessed'? How will that be done and by whom (e.g. the work could be displayed as an exhibition and comments made by visitors and peers)?

- How will you showcase your work at the end of this project?

- How will you archive and share this work?

Look and think before opening the shutter.
The heart and mind are the true lens of the camera.

Yousuf Karsh

Suggested themes

The idea of a photo essay based around their lives is quite straightforward, but could be expanded or split into themes and linked with different areas of the curriculum. For example:

- The weather, seasons, nature, light, water, etc.

- Local area or town/city

- Issues (e.g. pollution, graffiti, bullying, zoos, healthy lifestyles)

- A person of a different generation (e.g. a grandparent)

- An event (e.g. birth of a child, wedding, award ceremony)

- Customs/celebrations (e.g. Halloween, Valentine's Day, May Day)

- Animals

- A building (e.g. supermarket, town hall, leisure centre, factory, museum)

- Jobs/roles

- Fashion

- A local team

- Food

James Mollison's book, *Where Children Sleep*, is a good starting point for discussions and to give the pupils some about ideas about taking a theme and transforming it into a series of photographs.[1] Mollison describes how, as a child, his bedroom was his personal kingdom – this is the key idea behind the book. Each double-page spread (the book is A4 and coffee-table style) includes, on the left-hand page, a photograph of a child in front of a neutral background with some detailed text, and on the right-hand page, a full-page shot of where the child sleeps.

Although the images show a range of cultures, wealth and backgrounds, the book is about so much more than simply showing the rich–poor divide. It would be wrong to think of the book as a simplistic portrayal of what poor children lack; instead, it provides an insight into the worlds of the children represented: a child who has to pass exams before they are allowed into school, a child who has a Saturday job to pay for her wigs, the child who has an ASBO, the child who practises her karate for four hours a day ... The children have such diverse lives that each image serves as a starting point for research and discussion. This could lead to dialogue which will provide pupils with a deeper awareness about how they might wish to depict themselves in their own photo essay.

See Chapter 7:
Visual literacy

---

1   J. Mollison, *Where Children Sleep* (London: Chris Boot, 2010).

Another source of inspiration is Gabriele Galimberti's Toy Stories, which consists of a series of images of children from around the world with their prized possessions.[2] The photographs demonstrate how all children 'play', regardless of where they live and how much money their parents have. The way that they play, and what they play with, reveals much about their lives and their aspirations.

You could also introduce the pupils to Peter Menzel's *Hungry Planet*, which is a photo essay of families from around the world, photographed with a week's supply of food on their table.[3] The images show the range of food and the volume eaten in clear visual terms. There are also notes on the cost and the favourite foods of each family.

These suggestions may give pupils some inspiration for their own work, but they will certainly provide the teacher with a series of starting points for discussions or models for a range of different approaches to the photo essay.

2   See <http://www.gabrielegalimberti.com/projects/toys-2/>.

3   P. Menzel and F. D'Aluisio, *Hungry Planet: What the World Eats* (Napa, CA: Material World Books, 2007). See also <http://www.time.com/time/photogallery/0,29307,1626519,00.html>.

Chapter 13

Quick wins

Independent learning which involves working outside of the classroom can be incorporated into many of the ideas in this chapter. The key to success with these activities is to remember that the camera is a powerful tool in the hands of children. As Wendy Ewald observes: 'Photography offers a language that can draw on the imagination in a way that we never thought possible before.'[1] Allow the pupils the freedom to see the world through their own eyes.

Photo booth

The current 'in thing' at weddings and events, in terms of photography, appears to be the 'photo booth'. This is based loosely around the old-fashioned kiosk we used to use for passport photos – where you would sit in front of a screen, look terrified and receive a strip of photos in which you are desperately trying not to pull a face. Now these are seen as 'fun booths' where you can pose for a series of images using a prop, like a fake moustache or a blackboard on which you write a message. As a nod to nostalgia, these can be printed off in a strip. The background to the photo booth is

---

1 W. Ewald, *I Wanna Take Me a Picture: Teaching Photography and Writing to Children* (Boston, MA: Beacon Press, 2001), p. 14.

often linked to the wedding theme but can be themed around anything.

Try building your own classroom photo booth using only junk, scrap or recycled materials, and ask the children to come up with some props to go with it. Just to put this into context and show how easily you can build something from junk, take a look at the image to the right of a 'time machine' that a group of enthusiastic pupils built with Nick Garnett (aka Red Van Man).[2]

Not only will pupils have great fun being resourceful and building the photo booth, but you can then put it into action and take images of other classes or staff members, or use it at a school event with pupils taking photographs of parents.

You could use your photo booth to take a head shot of everyone in the class, print and laminate the images and put them into a box – you could then pull one out when choosing who will answer a question.

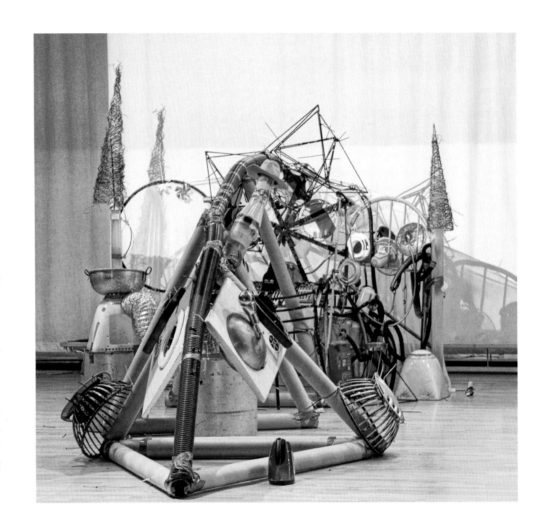

2 See <www.redvanman.net>.

Time capsule

Set the pupils the task of designing a time capsule (the materials used will be dependent on where it is going to be stored) which they will then fill with thirty images – these must sum up your school clearly. When will the capsule be opened? Who will be the audience (is it yourselves in five years' time or pupils from your school in fifty years' time)?

You could create your time capsule with your class in September to be opened in July of the same academic year. If that is the case, you don't need to worry about your photographs fading or disintegrating. You are unlikely to bury it so it does not need to be airtight, and as you will be the one who is opening it, you will not need a map to find it!

If, however, you are creating a time capsule for your whole school or community and one that you want to open in, say 2050, you and your pupils will need to consider storage issues carefully and do some scientific research around preserving photographs and creating a durable capsule. Think about rubber bands or staples – will they perish and leave marks? How can you ensure the photographs will remain intact?

You can develop this activity as far as you want. The International Time Capsule Society will allow you to register your capsule to ensure that it will not be forgotten or the exact whereabouts lost.[3]

---

3   See <http://www.oglethorpe.edu/about_us/crypt_of_civilization/international_ time_capsule_society.asp>.

Alphabet of bodies

Ask the pupils to create a photographic alphabet using only their bodies to make the letters! This is a fun activity but one that will also encourage team work. Where will they take the photographs? Is the background important? What about the angle from which they will take the images? What will they wear in the photos? The pupils might want to think about wearing all-black clothing (e.g. black leggings and black t-shirt) so the images are more striking.

They might also want to consider what they could create with their series of photographs. For example, they could create a resource for very young pupils to help them learn the alphabet and then discuss how they would actually present this to them. Alternatively, they could produce a book, a poster, a set of flash cards or a movie.

> Create a freeze-frame which shows a particular emotion or concept.
>
> This could be photographed and then projected onto a screen to see if the rest of the class can work out the concept – a bit like Pictionary with bodies! Ideas for emotions might include: tired, confused, helpful, lost, frightened and curious.

Philosophical discussions

Photographs are great for provoking discussions but sometimes it's not the actual photograph itself that is important but what it aims to capture. For example, the question 'Can you take the same photograph twice?' was suggested by a Year 10 pupil. Another pupil immediately said, 'Of course you can – just press the shutter' (which produced a few eye-rolls and 'durs'!). Undeterred, the poser of the question disagreed, and insisted: 'How can it be the same – something will always have changed?'

The pupils then came up with the following ideas:

- Lighting, time of day, time of year, angle and camera settings can all change.

- We can control some of these qualities (e.g. we could deliberately choose the settings), but if the light is different then the same settings will produce a different photo.

- If there is a person in the photo, their clothes, hair, facial expressions can all change. (You might want to bring in the quote from *Alice in Wonderland* here: 'I can't go back to yesterday because I was a different person then.')

They pushed it then and said: 'OK, let's put the shutter on continuous and take two photos – one a fraction of a second after the other. Surely these would be the same photo?' However careful you are, though, you will always get a slight 'ghosting' if you put on top of each other two supposedly identical images taken in a shutter burst. So, if the person has moved slightly or they are a second older, is it the same photo?

> Try and take the same photograph twice! Examine your results.

Some pupils tried to create identical images and the discussion continued. Eventually we decided that no, you can't take the same photo twice. Your pupils might think differently though!

To further the discussion, you could look at 'Natalie Time Lapse: Birth to Ten Years Old in 1 min 25 seconds'.[4] A father has taken a photo of his daughter every day for ten years and then put the images together in a movie and played it at high speed. Tiny changes which would be unnoticeable on a daily basis become breathtaking when speeded up.

> Is a photograph still a photograph even if it is never printed?

---

4   Natalie Time Lapse: Birth to 10 Years Old in 1 minute 25 seconds. Available at: <http://www.youtube.com/watch?v=ejbNVWES4LI>. Or take a look at the series of self-portraits by Argentine photographer Sophie Starzenski which were taken throughout her pregnancy: <http://www.theguardian.com/artanddesign/gallery/2013/nov/15/pictures-of-week-day-pregnancy-selfies>/.

Can you take the same photograph twice?

Recreate famous paintings

Choose a selection of famous paintings – you can put these into a slide show or print them off and place in sealed envelopes. In groups, the pupils are allocated a painting. Their task is to interpret and recreate their own version of it as a photograph. It doesn't have to be exactly the same – the photograph is merely a starting point.

For example, most of us know what Edvard Munch's painting *The Scream* looks like. How could this be rendered? What sort of questions do pupils need to ask? What background will they use? Will they locate or create a background? Will they take the photograph indoors or outdoors? Will they use any props? If props are to be used, will they make them or borrow them? Will it be a straightforward photograph or one that is that is edited to make it appear as 'abstract' as *The Scream?*

Create an exhibition of the pupils' images, perhaps with a print of the original painting alongside the pupils' version. Alternatively, display the photos with no titles – other children and staff could be asked to work out which paintings are being portrayed.

You could take this further and ask pupils to do the original research to find a famous painting which they would like to recreate.

Mosaic images

In groups of four, pupils should take four head shots – one of each person. They should then print these out and cut them into four. They can then mix up the images to create four new faces. How do they feel about the images they have created?

Perspective

Working in groups, the pupils should choose a subject – it can be anything, such as a person, an object or a view. They should take three images of their subject from different angles. They can then turn these into a triptych using online software, an app or just printing them out and displaying them on one sheet of paper.

> Choose a member of staff (not necessarily a teacher) and create a 'photo story' of their day. You can only use a maximum of nine images so think carefully and plan.

*There is a vast difference between taking a
picture and making a photograph.*

Robert Heinecken

Forced perspective

Perspective literally means 'your view' – it can be a physical view (i.e. what is in front of you) or your stance on something (i.e. your take on an idea or a subject). By being creative with the placing of objects and people, it is possible to create images which alter our perspective. If you think back to the old B movies, in which plastic-looking monsters stomped through the streets, this was achieved by placing the model of the monster much closer to the camera than the people, thus playing with our sense of scale. The most famous forced perspective images are the tourist photographs taken at sites like the Leaning Tower of Pisa, where the person in the image is standing in such a way that it looks as if they are holding up the tower.[5]

Get the pupils to go outside and find a suitable space to create their own forced perspective images. One of the easiest is to take a photograph where it appears that a pupil is standing on the hand of another, as in the images opposite.

In order to recreate this, find a fairly empty space – if you can find a slope, so much the better. Place the person holding out their hand close to the camera and then direct the other person to stand several paces behind so that they are in line with the person's hand. You can do this with just one hand or two. Once you see how the technique works you can be creative with poses – for example, make it look as if the person in front is picking up the person behind by having them pinch their fingers and the person behind extend their arm upwards to be in line with the fingers.

You can experiment with buildings – for example, have the pupil position their hand so that it looks as if they are holding the top of the building (this naturally leads to work on scale). Or use plastic dinosaur figures to create your own movie posters for 'the revenge of the dinosaurs' or other corny movie ideas!

---

5   If you search the Internet for 'forced perspective images' you will find hundreds of examples, or check out <http://www. environmentalgraffiti.com/featured/not-photoshopped-incredible-forced-perspective-photography/14968?image=6>.

Discussions and surveys

Pose a question to the pupils: why do people take photographs? They should discuss and write an answer to this in no more than 100 words. They may wish to undertake a survey and ask other people for their opinions before writing this.

> 'I hate having my photograph taken.' Why do you think so many people say this?
>
> What is our 'self-image' and how different is it to how others see us?

Colour

Divide the class into groups and give each group a colour. They must then take multiple images which are predominantly of that colour. It will make it easier if they fill the viewfinder with their image. They should then create one large image from their smaller ones. These large images can then be placed side by side. Use these as a discussion starter for how colour suggests mood and how colour is used in imagery and advertising. You could take this further and ask the pupils to write poetry or similes based on these colourful images.

Zoopraxiscope

The zoopraxiscope was invented by Eadweard Muybridge in 1879.[6] In very basic terms, a zoopraxiscope projects images from rapidly rotating discs to give the impression of motion. It is therefore a very primitive film projector and is thought to have been the inspiration for film pioneers such as Thomas Edison. Muybridge created the first zoopraxiscope in order to try to prove that when a horse is running quickly, all four of its hooves leave the ground.

This could be a joint science, ICT and DT project in which pupils create their zoopraxiscope after doing some research on Muybridge.

---

6 For more information on Muybridge visit <http://www.eadweardmuybridge.co.uk/>.

Shape Collage

Shape Collage[7] can be used as an app or as a Windows/Mac program. It is free to download and is very straightforward to use. You add as many images as you wish and then choose your shape. There are pre-loaded shapes, such as rectangles and hearts, but there is an option to upload your own shape or image as a background template. You can also turn your images into text. This is great for creating a memory of a special event. The heart example on the right was created for a primary school which was about to become an academy and wanted to create some memories.

Here are some other ideas you could try out with pupils:

- Choose a theme (e.g. nature) and then use a suitable shape (such as a flower) as your template.

- Select the heart shape as your template and ask pupils to take images based around 'What we love about our school/town/local area'.

- Select the text option and ask pupils to use either self-portraits or images which represent them and place these into the shape of their name.

7 See <http://www.shapecollage.com>.

Sun print images

Select the text option to create your school name and ask pupils to take images from around school. The resulting work could be displayed in reception, on publicity materials or as blog headers.

Ask pupils to pick an event or theme and compile related images into one word of text. (See the 'risk' example below which was generated during a TeachMeet based around the idea of taking risks.)

Using sun print, or light sensitive, paper get the pupils to create their own images using just natural light. By positioning objects on the paper and then placing this in direct sunlight, the shape of the object will appear as a silhouette directly on the paper. By 'fixing' this with water for a couple of minutes, you then have a permanent image to display. If the pupils then take photographs of their created images, they can alter the colours and create a whole different feel to their photographs.

Sun print paper

Immediate effect

Image 'fixed with water

Image 'solarised' using software

Aged photographs

Artificially aged photographs can be deployed in many curriculum areas, not just history. For example, if pupils are creating a diary or information pack which sums up a person's life, or if they are using a photo as a clue to a mystery or detective quest, then taking a modern image and manipulating it is now really easy to do. In the past (as many of you will know from experience), making an image look old involved using tea bags and coffee splatters or, if you were very brave, burning the edges or making holes in the photograph. The modern equivalent of 'tea bagging' is to use an app such as Strut Type or Pic Grunger.

With Strut Type, it is possible to control the colour of the image, ranging through from sepia to salt lemon. You can add differing types of decay, including peeling, mildew, mould and stains. You can then finalise your image with light leaks for different shades and add a border. The end result is very effective, especially if you crumple up the image after printing or tear it in places. You could create an aged image yourself and use it as a stimulus or get pupils to create the stimulus image themselves and then write the 'mystery' around the image.

Colours

Mould and Peeling

Aged effects

Photography letters

Ask pupils to take twenty-six images of letters of the alphabet but be as creative as possible. For example, are there branches of a tree shaped like a letter? Is there a parking symbol that could represent P? Can they zoom in on an individual letter on a signpost? They could then create an alphabet poster with their photos.

Free choice

Allow pupils to create their own photography challenge! If you have already tried out some of the examples in this book with your classes, they should now have the confidence and the curiosity to take on this challenge. Perhaps share with them this quote from photographer Imogen Cunningham: 'Which of my photographs is my favourite? The one I'm going to take tomorrow.'

Light leaks

Borders

Which of my photographs is my favourite?
The one I'm going to take tomorrow.

Imogen Cunningham

Thanks and acknowledgements

I would like to thank the following:

Ellis Primary School, Hoyland Common Primary School, Shafton Primary School, Worsbrough Common Primary School and Greenacre Special School for their help in testing ideas and materials.

Phlegm, the street artist from Sheffield, for allowing me to photograph and use his creations.

Balasz Gardi for kindly allowing me free use of his iPhone image on page 59.

Ben Heine for kindly allowing use of his image on page 112.

Markland Hill Primary School, Bolton, for kindly allowing me to use Troy's 100-word story on page 118.

To numerous friends and family for 'loaning' me your children to photograph and for allowing their images to be used in this book.

With special thanks to:

Hywel Roberts for paving the way, giving me confidence and showing me how to be 'brave'.

Matthew Milburn for pushing me out of my comfort zone and believing in me.

The amazing staff throughout the years at Kingstone School and the Dearne Advanced Learning Centre, in Barnsley, for their never-ending support through laughter and tears. There are too many of you to name individually but you know who you are and how inspirational you all are.

All my family and friends, but especially my mum and dad – I owe you everything.

Caroline, Bev, Rosalie, Emma, Tom and everyone at Crown House Publishing for their support and care – you are wonderful people.

My Twitter #photochallenge friends for providing encouragement and light relief through the time spent writing this book.

A special thanks to Susan and Brian – you have supported me so much through the years. Long may our friendship continue.

My wonderful sons, Adam and Matthew, for shaping me into the person I am today – I love you both very much.

Finally, my amazingly patient, supportive, bag-carrying assistant photographer and driver, aka my husband, Tony.

Words aren't enough, but thank you all.

About the author

Jane Hewitt taught, mainly at secondary level, for 30 years. She still loves learning, discovering new ideas and photography and is rarely found without a camera around her neck.

Jane is a talented photographer, unless where specified all photographs in this book were taken by her.

Bibliography

Bamford, A. (2003). Visual Literacy White Paper. Available at: <http://wwwimages.adobe.com/www.adobe.com/content/dam/Adobe/en/education/pdfs/visual-literacy-wp.pdf>.

BBC (2000). Papers Defy Advert Ban (22 January). Available at: <http://news.bbc.co.uk/1/hi/uk/614319.stm>.

Beever, J. (2010). *Pavement Chalk Artist: The Three Dimensional Drawings of Julian Beever* (New York: Firefly Books).

Blackburn, K. and Schirillo, J. (2012). Emotive Hemispheric Differences Measured in Real-Life Portraits Using Pupil Diameter and Subjective Aesthetic Preferences, *Experimental Brain Research* 219(4): 447–455.

Bolam, R. (2013). 100 Years of Stainless Steel: Faunagraphic Mural of Harry Brearley [video]. Available at: <https://vimeo.com/65722308>.

Bowen, J. (2012). *A Street Cat Named Bob: How One Man and His Cat Found Hope on the Streets* (London: Hodder & Stoughton).

Bracey, J. (2012). The War on Film, *Photography Monthly* (11 October). Available at: <http://www.photographymonthly.com/Magazine/Photography-Monthly-articles/Interview-with-photography-legend-Don-McCullin>.

Clark, D. (2010). Casualties of War – David Turnley – Icons of Photography, *Amateur Photographer* (27 February). Available at: <http://www.amateurphotographer.co.uk/how-to/icons-of-photography/535927/casualties-of-war-david-turnley-icons-of-photography>.

Coomes, P. (2013). Thatcher's Funeral: The View from Above, *BBC News* (23 April). Available at: <http://www.bbc.co.uk/news/in-pictures-22225122>.

Debes, J. (1968). Some Foundations for Visual Literacy, *Audiovisual Instruction* 13: 961–964.

Ewald, W. (2001). *I Wanna Take Me a Picture: Teaching Photography and Writing to Children* (Boston, MA: Beacon Press).

Fabbri, G., Fabbri, M. and Wilkund, P. (2009). *From Pinhole to Print: Inspiration, Instructions and Insights in Less Than an Hour* (Stockholm: Alternative Photography).

Finger, B. (2011). *13 Photos Children Should Know* (London: Prestel).

Finger, B. (2012). *50 Photos You Should Know* (London: Prestel).

Giorgis, C., Johnson, N. J., Bonomo, A., Colbert, C., Conner, A. and Kauffman, G. (1999). Visual Literacy, *Reading Teacher* 53(2): 146–153.

Guardian (2011). War Photography? Isn't There An App for That? (7 July). Available at: <http://www.guardian.co.uk/media/2011/jul/06/afghanistan-war-iphone-images>.

Huntington, F. (2012). *The Burning House: What Would You Take?* (New York: HarperCollins).

Jones, T. (2012). *Dear Photograph* (New York: HarperCollins).

Junod, T. (2009). The Falling Man, *Esquire* (8 September). Available at: <http://www.esquire.com/features/ESQ0903-SEP_FALLINGMAN>.

Loyd, A. (2012). Don McCullin: My Last War, *The Times Magazine* (29 December). Available at: <http://www.thetimes.co.uk/tto/magazine/article3638191.ece>.

Marinovich, G. and Silva, J. (2000). *The Bang-Bang Club: Snapshots from a Hidden War* (London: William Heinemann).

McCullin, D. (1992). *Unreasonable Behaviour: An Autobiography* (London: Vintage).

McCullin, D. (1994). *Sleeping With Ghosts: A Life's Work in Photography* (London: Vintage).

Menzel, P. and D'Aluisio, F. (2007). *Hungry Planet: What the World Eats* (Napa, CA: Material World Books).

Moeller, S. (1999). *Compassion Fatigue: How the Media Sell Disease, Famine, War and Death* (London and New York: Routledge).

Mollison, J. (2010). *Where Children Sleep* (London: Chris Boot).

Peterson, B. (2008). *Understanding Shutter Speed: Creative Action and Low-Light Photography Beyond 1/125 Second* (New York: Amphoto).

Pompeo, J. (2011). Photographer Behind 9/11 'Falling Man' Retraces Steps, Recalls 'Unknown Soldier', *Yahoo! News* (29 August). Available at: <http://news.yahoo.com/photographer-behind-9-11-falling-man-retraces-steps-recalls-unknown-soldier.html>.

Roberts, S. C. (2011). *The Art of iPhoneography: A Shutter Sister's Guide to Mobile Creativity* (Lewes: Ilex Press).

Romany, W. G. (2011). *Beauty in Decay: The Art of Urban Exploration* (Darlington: Carpet Bombing Culture).

Shaw, M. J. and Sutcliffe, F. M. (2002). *Every Now and Then* (Whitby: Sutcliffe Gallery).

Shove, G. (ed.) (2010). *Untitled III: This is Street Art* (Darlington: Carpet Bombing Culture).

Slinkachu (2008). *Little People in the City: The Street Art of Slinkachu* (London: Boxtree).

Slinkachu and Jenkins, M. (2009). Little Wonders, *The Guardian* (4 April). Available at: <http://www.theguardian.com/travel/2009/apr/04/slinkachu-street-art-graffiti-britain>.

Syed, M. (2010). *Bounce: The Myth of Talent and the Power of Practice* (London: Fourth Estate).

Time (2011). 50 Websites That Make the Web Great (16 August). Available at: <http://content.time.com/time/specials/packages/article/0,28804,2087815_2087868_2087873,00.html>.

van Agtmael, P. (2013). Revisiting Memory and Preserving Legacy: Tim Hetherington and Chris Hondros (18 April). Available at: <http://lightbox.time.com/2013/04/18/revisiting-memory-and-preserving-legacy-tim-hetherington-and-chris-hondros/>.

Warner Marien, M. (2012). *100 Ideas that Changed Photography* (London: Laurence King).

Index

Activity   Software or app   Technical information   Curriculum or subject area

Activity Software or app Technical information Curriculum or subject area